THE SOCIAL ROLE OF
THE MAN OF KNOWLEDGE

COLUMBIA UNIVERSITY LECTURES
JULIUS BEER FOUNDATION

THE SOCIAL ROLE
OF THE
MAN OF KNOWLEDGE

By FLORIAN ZNANIECKI

NEW YORK

COLUMBIA UNIVERSITY PRESS

1940

COPYRIGHT 1940
COLUMBIA UNIVERSITY PRESS, NEW YORK

Foreign Agents: OXFORD UNIVERSITY PRESS, Humphrey Milford, Amen House, London, E.C. 4, England, AND B. I. Building, Nicol Road, Bombay, India; MARUZEN COMPANY, LTD., 6 Nihonbashi, Tori-Nichome, Tokyo, Japan

MANUFACTURED IN THE UNITED STATES OF AMERICA

TO COLUMBIA UNIVERSITY
THAT WORLD-FAMOUS ASSOCIATION
OF PRESENT AND FUTURE LEADERS IN
EVERY KIND AND EVERY FIELD OF KNOWLEDGE
THIS WORK IS HUMBLY DEDICATED

CONTENTS

I. SOCIOLOGY AND THEORY OF KNOWLEDGE   1

II. TECHNOLOGISTS AND SAGES   23

III. SCHOOLS AND SCHOLARS AS BEARERS OF ABSOLUTE TRUTH   91

IV. THE EXPLORER AS CREATOR OF NEW KNOWLEDGE   164

INDEX   201

CHAPTER ONE

SOCIOLOGY AND THEORY OF KNOWLEDGE

Sociology is still young and inclined to be imperialistic. Her forefathers claimed for her the entire domain of culture, and many of her faithful courtiers are trying to make those claims good by extending her sway over the fields of law, economics, technology, language, literature, art, religion, knowledge. These attempts conflict not only with the vested rights of the sciences that have of old dominated these fields but also with the counter-claims of sociology's equally aggressive rival—psychology, which is in turn encroaching upon sociological grounds. The resultant struggles have not been unproductive. New problems have been defined, new methods devised for their solution. On the other hand, however, many strictly sociological problems are still neglected or treated inadequately. It is all very well to cultivate the borderlands between the special sciences, but each science should first cultivate properly its own field by its own methods.

We are concerned here with that particular set of borderland problems that has recently been termed the "sociology of knowledge"—a term parallel to "sociology of religion," "sociology of art," "sociology of language." Interest in these problems goes back to the very beginnings of modern sociological thought. The central idea of Comte's famous "law of three states" was that between certain types of philosophy or—more generally—of knowledge (theological, metaphysical, positive) and certain forms of social structure there exists a relationship of mutual dependence. Half a century later, the French sociological group centered around Durkheim tried in a series of highly significant studies to show the social origin of the fundamental forms of human experience and thinking.[1] More recently, German sociologists, especially Max Scheler and Karl Mannheim, have made systematic efforts to trace the dependence of knowledge on social conditions.[2]

The term "sociology of knowledge" seems to us rather

[1] See Émile Durkheim, *Les Formes élémentaires de la vie religieuse* (Paris, Alcan, 1912), for a general outline of the sociological approach to knowledge. E. Durkheim and Marcel Mauss in "Des quelques formes primitives de la classification," *Année sociologique VI,* show cases in which logical classes are determined by the subdivision of social groups. Lucien Lévy-Bruhl in his famous series of works on primitive thinking, *Les Fonctions mentales dans les sociétés inferieures* (Alcan, 1910), *La Mentalité primitive* (1922), *L'Ame primitive* (1927), *Le Surnaturel et la nature dans la mentalité primitive* (1931), *L'Expérience mystique et les symboles chez les primitifs* (1930), tends to prove that "primitive"—or rather "preliterate" (Faris)—peoples use logical principles and categories different from ours: the obvious suggestion is that both theirs and ours are socially conditioned. Maurice Halbwachs in *Les Cadres sociaux de la mémoire* (Paris, Alcan, 1924) shows that our memory, and consequently also our experience of time, is organized by a socially established and regulated framework of succession and simultaneity within which the facts of collective life are fitted. S. Czarnowski applied the sociological approach to space, particularly in his monograph "Le Morcellement de l'étendue," *Revue de l'histoire des religions,* 1927.

[2] Cf. M. Scheler, ed., *Versuche zu einer Soziologie des Wissens* (1924) and *Die Wissensformen und die Gesellschaft* (1926); K. Mannheim, *Ideology and Utopia* (trans. Wirth and Shils, 1936); Mannheim's article, "Wissenssoziologie," in Vierkandt's *Handwörterbuch der Soziologie.*

unfortunate, for it suggests that knowledge as such is an object matter of sociological investigation. Now, every science deals with a specific class of systems and of processes. Sociology is primarily concerned with that class of systems which is called "social" (for example, a "social group," a "social relation") and with processes which occur within or between such systems. The distinctive characteristic of social systems is that their chief components are interacting men, whereas systems of knowledge, or theories (using this term in the most general sense), are obviously not social systems. Nor are linguistic, aesthetic, religious, or technical systems "social": there is little similarity between a compound sentence, a poem, a painting, a sacrifice, an automobile, on the one hand, and a political party, a club, a conjugal or parental relation, on the other hand, beyond the fact that each of them has an inner order holding its constituent parts together.

Of course, between social systems on the one hand and other kinds of cultural systems on the other hand there are many dynamic relationships of one-sided or mutual dependence, some of which we are going to investigate presently. But there are likewise relationships of dependence between other kinds of systems. If the existence of such relationships entitles us to use the terms "sociology of knowledge" and "sociology of art," by the same token we should be justified in speaking of "linguistics of religion," "religionistics of art," "economics of knowledge," and so on.

However, there is no need of wrangling about words.

Since the expression "sociology of knowledge" has by now gained a wide recognition in sociological literature, we may as well adopt it with the emphatic reservation that it does not mean a "sociological theory of knowledge." [3] Otherwise, sociology would find itself in a curious position. As a theory of knowledge, a "science of the sciences," it would have to determine its own character as sociology; whereas as sociology it would determine its own character as a "science of the sciences." [4]

Many misunderstandings might be avoided if we had a fully constituted "science of knowledge," a comparative, inductive study of the various systems of knowledge which empirical research would disclose in the past and the present. Ever since antiquity, there has been indeed philosophy of knowledge—epistemology, logic, and methodology—trying to establish the general principles and norms upon which the validity of all knowledge depends, just as there has been a political and an ethical philosophy of social life. However, a science of knowledge parallel to modern sociology or linguistics would not attempt to standardize normatively the systems it studies but would view them simply as empirical realities, trying to reach by their comparative analysis theoretic generalizations about them. Such a science has only begun to emerge out of historical and ethnological studies. Its development is apparently a slow and difficult

[3] I am borrowing this distinction from an unpublished paper by Mr. Edwin Anderson on Durkheim's sociological approach to knowledge.

[4] Cf. Alexander von Schelting's criticism of Mannheim, *American Sociological Review*, August, 1936.

SOCIOLOGY AND KNOWLEDGE

task, and the sociologist is hardly competent to participate in it.[5]

For an objective investigation of systems of knowledge in their composition, structure, and relationships must take fully into consideration that which is an essential characteristic of every system of knowledge: its claim to be *true,* that is, objectively valid. The sociologist, however, is not entitled to make any judgments concerning the validity of any systems of knowledge except sociological systems. He meets systems of knowledge in the course of his investigation only when he finds that certain persons or groups that he studies are actively interested in them, that they construct, improve, supplement, reproduce, defend, or popularize systems which they regard as true or else reject, oppose, criticize, or interfere with the propagation of systems which they consider untrue. In every such case the sociologist is bound to abide by whatever standards of validity those individuals or groups apply to the knowledge in which they take an active share. For, as an observer of cultural life, he can understand the data he observes only if he takes them with the "humanistic coefficient," only if he does not limit his observation to his own direct experience of the data but reconstructs the experience of the men who are dealing with them actively.[6] Just as a conjugal rela-

---

[5] One of the most interesting coöperative efforts to build such a science from monographic contributions is represented by twenty volumes of the periodical *Nauka Polska* (Polish Science), S. Michalski, ed., Warsaw, 1920–39.

[6] F. Znaniecki, *The Method of Sociology* (New York, 1934).

tion which he observes is to him really and objectively what it is to the conjugal partners themselves, or an association what it means to its members, a given system of knowledge must be to him also what it is to the people who participate in its construction, reproduction, application, and development. When he is studying their social lives, he must agree that, as to the knowledge which they recognize as valid, they are the only authority he need consider. He has no right as a sociologist to oppose his authority to theirs: he is bound by the methodical rule of unconditional modesty. He must resign his own criteria of theoretic validity when dealing with systems of knowledge which they accept and apply. It does not matter whether the type of knowledge which he finds these people cultivating be technical, normative or theoretic, theological, metaphysical or empirical, deductive or inductive, physical or humanistic, nor whether the particular system which they regard as true be the physics of Thales, of Democritus, of St. Thomas, of Newton, or of Einstein, the biology of Aristotle or of Darwin, the psychology of Plato or of the behaviorists: it is their judgment, not the sociologist's, which conditions whatever influence their knowledge has on their social life, and vice versa.

But how ought the sociologist behave when he finds that some people deny the validity of a system which other people regard as true? Does not this conflict of authorities compel him to make a decision? We do not think so. If we apply consistently the humanistic coefficient, we shall conclude that when a man takes a negative attitude toward a system of knowledge which others recognize, this is only a more or less interesting fact of his personal life, not affecting at all the objective composition, structure, or validity of the system which he rejects. In the same way, the fact that a person does not like the English language, impressionism in painting, or Calvinism in religion is entirely irrelevant to the intrinsic pattern and significance of those cultural systems as experienced by their adherents. Such a negative valuation may, however, be instructive in other respects. If a man rejects, for example, voluntaristic psychology because he applies to it the standards of behavioristic psychology which he recognizes as true, this fact (though it has no bearing upon voluntarism) throws light on the composition, structure, and claims to validity of behaviorism. In the same way, we learn something significant about the French language from the fact that some people do not like English because they judge it by French standards, or about the aesthetic pattern of cubism from a cubist who criticizes impressionism.

Let us accept as a "truth" any element of any system of knowledge taken with its humanistic coefficient, that is, taken from the standpoint of the men who believe that they understand this system, who are actively interested in it and regard it as containing objectively valid knowledge about the object matter to which it refers. How should such elements be defined? The sociologist is unable to answer this question; for the people who are actively interested in systems of knowledge variously conceive the nature of a "truth." "Truths" have been identified with names, sentences, propositions, artificial symbols and their relationships, ideas, representations, observations, concepts, judgments, intuitions, habits, responses to stimuli, and so on, and every such class may be variously defined; thus an "idea" of Plato's differs widely from an "idea" of Locke's. In observing, however, the actual functioning of these multiform "truths" in the sphere of active experience of the people who regard them as valid—in observing the influence which the recognition of certain truths has upon the conscious lives of people as experiencing and active subjects—we can say generally that whatever is regarded as a truth functions as a *norm of thinking,* imposes upon the conscious agent who recognizes it a distinctive selection and organization of some data of his experience. The data acquire thereby the character of object matter of knowledge. The "truth" itself—and even more so the whole system of which it is an element—possesses in the active experience of all those who recognize it an "objective" significance which makes its validity seem to them independent of their "subjective" emotions, wishes, representations. They *participate* in a system of knowledge, just as a leader or a member participates in a social group, a manager or a workman in that technical system which is called a "factory" or a "workshop."

Now, sociological investigation discovers that there are two kinds of connection between knowledge and social life. On the one hand, upon men's participation in a certain system of knowledge often depends their par-

SOCIOLOGY AND KNOWLEDGE

ticipation in some social system and their conduct within the limits of the latter. A person who is "instructed" or "learned" in certain theories is admitted to the performance of certain roles and to the membership of certain groups in which the "ignorant" are not allowed to share. A man who accepts the traditionalism of sacred, religious lore behaves differently as a member or functionary of particular groups from a man who recognizes the teleological rationalism of applied secular knowledge. The development and popularization of modern physical and biological sciences have markedly affected the composition and structure of many social groups, either directly by changing traditional beliefs or indirectly by the technological applications of those sciences.

On the other hand, the participation of men in certain social systems often determines (though perhaps not entirely or exclusively) in what systems of knowledge they will participate, and how. Many social groups require that all their members know certain sacred doctrines or the rudiments of some lay sciences, while some groups forbid their members to meddle with certain theories. Men who are destined for professional occupations must acquire the knowledge regarded as necessary for those occupations according to social rules and regulations. And there are various socially prescribed ways of participating in systems of knowledge. Sometimes men are expected and taught merely to memorize formulas in which knowledge is expressed, whereas at other times understanding of all the implications of a system is required. Exclusive emphasis may be put upon the practical application of the "truths" included in a system or, on the contrary, upon their purely theoretic significance. In many cases no modification of the system is allowed; in other cases it is regarded as not only permissible but meritorious to improve, develop, modify, supplement a system and in rare cases even to construct a new system.

Individual conformity with the various social demands relative to knowledge is obtained by specific methods of education, encouragement, and control. The success or failure of these methods in particular cases is conditioned, of course, by the psychological capacities and dispositions of the individuals to whom they are applied. But why individuals manifest such psychological capacities and dispositions as they possess by participating the way they do in certain systems of knowledge and not in others is a question which can be answered only by a study of the society in which those individuals live.

Thus, while admittedly systems of knowledge—viewed in their objective composition, structure, and validity—cannot be reduced to social facts, yet their historical existence within the empirical world of culture, in so far as it depends upon the men who construct them, maintain them by transmission and application, develop them, or neglect them, must in a large measure be explained sociologically. And this is what "sociology of knowledge" has actually been doing, whenever it was not vainly trying to become epistemology. Even thus limited, the task is sufficiently vast and difficult to occupy many sociologists for generations to come, especially as the con-

SOCIOLOGY AND KNOWLEDGE

ceptual framework hitherto used in dealing with these problems seems rather inadequate.

In our present outline we attempt to survey a certain portion of the field which "sociology of knowledge" tends to cover. We assume from experience and observation, direct and indirect, that knowledge as it has historically grown is the agglomerated product of specific cultural activities of numberless human individuals. Further, we are familiar with the fact that some individuals for longer or shorter periods of their lives specialize in cultivating knowledge, in distinction from other individuals who specialize in performing various other kinds of cultural activities—technical, economic, artistic, and so on. We call them "scientists," using the word in its etymological sense as derived from *scire,* "to know," and equivalent to "men of knowledge" (like the French term "savants"). This is obviously a different and much more extensive meaning than that in which this word is used by epistemologists and logicians, who define a "scientist" in terms of objective achievements in the field of knowledge. According to a conception prevalent in modern literature on the subject, an individual in order to be a scientist must produce some work which will qualify positively when judged by definite standards of validity. There are many writers who identify such standards with those of modern physical knowledge, to whom "science" means mathematics, astronomy, physics, and chemistry, with some portions of biology and perhaps geology grudgingly added; to them a "scientist" is only someone who efficiently works in one of those fields. Of course, as has been stated above, to us as sociologists, applying the humanistic coefficient to our data, all knowledge is valid which is regarded as such by the people who participate in it, and a "scientist" is any individual who is regarded by his social milieu and who regards himself as specializing in the cultivation of knowledge, irrespective of the positive or negative judgment which epistemologists or logicians may pronounce upon his work.

Now, individual specialization in any kind of cultural activity is generally recognized as a phenomenon which is socially conditioned. Sociologists have given considerable attention to it. Spencer was the first to treat it systematically in his *Principles of Sociology,* though we find some of his views anticipated in earlier works in social philosophy. For the most part, however, the attention of sociologists has centered upon the collective aspect of this phenomenon; viewing society as a whole, they regard individual specialization as a question of social structure, a differentiation of the total set of activities by which society is maintained. This is, for instance, what Durkheim emphasizes in his famous work *De la division du travail social,* in which progressive differentiation of functions is treated as the most significant collective process in the history of human societies.

But specialization has also an individual aspect: the persons who specialize in any kind of activity can be comparatively studied, irrespective of the part this activity plays in the total structure of a group or of society at large. Such studies may be psychological or sociological. In the former, attention centers upon the individual himself as a psychobiological being viewed apart from his social environment, and the problem is whether any typical psychological characteristics are associated with specialization in the given kind of activity and, if so, how this association is to be explained. There have been many monographic studies of this type in the course of the last half century, and they have been greatly stimulated by the development of psychotechnics and of vocational guidance, the purpose of which is to select for definite occupations individuals who possess or can easily develop the psychological characteristics which these occupations are supposed to require. In sociological studies of specialized persons, it is the connection between the individual and his social milieu which is the main object of interest; and his specialized activities are viewed with reference to the cultural setting in which they are performed. A classical example is Frazer's study of priests and kings in *The Golden Bough* (1935, Vols. I and II). Of course, a particular investigation may combine psychological and sociological problems, as exemplified in Sombart's monograph *Der Bourgeois*.

In sociology a conceptual framework for dealing with these problems has been gradually developing in the course of monographic investigations. In recent years the term "social role" has been used by many sociologists to denote the phenomena in question.[7] We say that a priest,

[7] Some sociologists prefer the term "personal role." The concept may be traced back to C. H. Cooley's *Human Nature and the Social Order*

a lawyer, a politician, a banker, a merchant, a physician, a farmer, a workman, a soldier, a housewife, a teacher performs a specific social role. Furthermore, the concept (with certain variations) has proved applicable not only to individuals who specialize in certain activities but also to individuals as members of certain groups: thus, an American, a Frenchman, a Methodist, a Catholic, a Communist, a Fascist, a club member, a member of the family (child, father, mother, grandparent) plays a certain social role.[8] An individual in the course of his life performs a number of different roles, successively or simultaneously; the synthesis of all the social roles he has ever performed from birth to death constitutes his social personality.

Every social role presupposes that between the individual performing the role, who may thus be called a "social person," and a smaller or larger set of people who participate in his performance and may be termed his "social circle" there is a common bond constituted by a complex of values which all of them appreciate posi-

---

(1902). R. E. Park, E. W. Burgess, G. H. Mead, E. T. Hiller, and others have developed it since then. In the form here presented, it has been utilized in a series of monographic investigations based on firsthand materials and carried on for a number of years by myself and my assistants. These investigations covered the following classes of social role: peasant, peasant housewife, farm laborer, industrial worker, unemployed worker, child in family, pupil in school, youthful member of playgroup, soldier, teacher, artist. Materials have been drawn in each case from several national societies. Some of these studies have been published, mostly in Polish. The first outline of the present study was published in the *Polish Sociological Review*, 1937.

[8] Cf. the author's "Social Groups as Products of Coöperating Individuals," *American Journal of Sociology*, May, 1939.

tively. These are economic values in the case of a merchant or a banker and the circle formed by his clients; hygienic values for the physician and his patients; political values for a king and his subjects; religious values for the priest and his circle of lay believers; aesthetic values for the artist and the circle of his admirers and critics; a combination of various values which fill the content of family life between the child and his family circle. The person is an object of positive valuation on the part of his circle because they believe that they all need his coöperation for the realization of certain tendencies connected with these values. The banker's coöperation is presumably needed by those who tend to invest or borrow money; the physician's coöperation by those who wish to regain or to preserve their own health and the health of the people in whom they are interested; the child's coöperation by other family members for the maintenance of family life. On the other hand, the person obviously cannot perform his role without the coöperation of his circle—though not necessarily the coöperation of any particular individual within the circle. There can be no active banker without clients, no practicing physician without patients, no reigning king without subjects, no child-in-the-family without other family members.

The person is conceived by his circle as an organic and psychological entity who is a "self," conscious of his own existence as a body and a soul and aware of how others regard him. If he is to be the kind of person his social circle needs, his "self" must possess in the opinion of the circle certain qualities, physical and mental, and not possess certain other qualities. For instance, organic "health" or "sickness" affects his supposed capacity to perform most roles, but particularly occupational roles, such as the farmer's, the workman's, the soldier's, and the housewife's, which require certain bodily skills; while lack of training in the "proper" ways of moving and eating may exclude an individual from roles which require "society" manners. Some roles are limited to men, others to women; there are upper or lower age limits for every role; the majority of roles imply certain somatic racial characteristics and definite, though variable, standards of external appearance.

The psychological qualities ascribed to persons performing social roles are enormously diversified: in every Western language there are hundreds of words denoting supposed traits of "intelligence" and "character"; and almost every such trait has, or had in the past, an axiological significance, that is, is positively or negatively valued, either in all persons or in persons performing certain kinds of role. In naïve popular reflection, such psychological traits are real qualities of a substantial "mind" or "soul," whose existence is manifested by specific acts (including verbal statements) of the individual.

A person who is needed by a social circle and whose self possesses the qualities required for the role for which he is needed has a definite social *status*, that is, his circle grants him certain rights and enforces those rights, when necessary, against individual participants of the circle or outsiders. Some of those rights concern his bodily existence. For instance, he has an ecological position, the right to occupy a definite space (as home, room, office, seat) where he is safe from bodily injury, and the right to move safely over given territories. His economic position includes rights to use certain material values regarded as necessary for his subsistence on a level commensurate with his role. Other rights involve his "spiritual welfare": he has a fixed moral standing, can claim some recognition, social response, and participation in the nonmaterial values of his circle.

He, in turn, has a social *function* to fulfill; he is regarded as obliged to achieve certain tasks by which the supposed needs of his circle will be satisfied and to behave toward other individuals in his circle in a way that shows his positive valuation of them.

Such are the essential components which we believe, on the basis of previous studies, to be found in all social roles, although of course the specific composition of different kinds of social role varies considerably. But our knowledge of a social role is not complete if we know only its composition, for a role is a dynamic system and its components may be variously interconnected in the course of its performance. There are many different ways of performing a role, according to the dominant active tendencies of the performer. He may, for instance, be mainly interested in one of the components of his role—the social circle, his own self, the status, or the function—and tend to subordinate other components to it. And, whatever his main interest, he may tend to conform with the demands of his circle or else try to innovate, to become independent of those demands. And, again, in either case he may be optimistically confident in the opportunities offered by his role and tend to expand it or else he may mistrust its possibilities and tend to restrict it to a perfectly secure minimum.

The possibility of reaching such general conclusions about all social roles and more specific, though still widely applicable, generalizations about social roles of a certain kind—such as the role of peasant, priest, merchant, factory worker, or artist—points obviously to the existence of essential uniformities and also of important variations among these social phenomena. Social roles constitute one general class of social system, and this class may be subdivided into less general classes, these into subclasses, and so on; for instance, within the specific class of factory worker there are hundreds of subclasses of workers employed in particular trades and there is another line of differentiation according to the economic organization of the factories in which they are employed. Systematic sociology stands before a task similar to that of systematic biology with its still greater complication of classes and subclasses of living organisms; and here, as there, only uniformities of specific systems make possible a further search for static and dynamic laws. But, manifestly, the source of uniformities in the social field is different from that in the field of biology.

Although in both fields differentiation is due to variations of individual systems, biological uniformities are due in the main to heredity; whereas uniformities of social systems, like those of all cultural systems, are chiefly the result of a reflective or unreflective use of the same *cultural patterns* in many particular cases. There is obviously a fundamental and universal, though unreflective, cultural pattern in accordance with which all kinds of lasting relationships between individuals and their social milieus are normatively organized and which we denote by the term "social role." The genesis of this pattern is lost in an inaccessible past, and so are the origins of what are probably its earliest variations, that is, those which everywhere differentiate individual roles according to sex and age.

But most of the patterns which have evolved during the history of mankind can be studied in the course of their becoming and duration. They originated usually by differentiation from older undifferentiated patterns, more seldom by entirely original, though gradual, invention. Many of these new patterns were short-lived or applied only within small collectivities, but some have lasted for thousands of years and spread over whole continents. In modern American society we find a number of patterns of social roles which can be traced back to prehistoric times, some still very vital, like the pattern of the rural housewife, others probably mere survivals destined soon to disappear, such as the patterns of the magician and the fortune teller.

Sometimes a pattern is explicitly formulated as a system of legal or ethical norms prescribing what all the roles of a given class within a particular political or religious society ought to be: such a pattern is then imposed by a dominant group upon all the candidates to those roles. For example, this is how the patterns of the several military, administrative, legislative, and judiciary roles are maintained and transmitted by state legislation; the patterns of priestly and medical roles are determined and stabilized in professional groups; the patterns of merchants' and artisans' roles in the Western world were perpetuated through centuries by the agency of guilds and corporations. In other cases, patterns of social roles are not explicitly rationalized but are included in the mores of a community and transmitted from old to young through a process of educational guidance and imitation; such has been the process of perpetuation of the role patterns of aristocrats, farmers, housewives, servants. Sometimes, again, mores have been supplemented and modified by normative group regulation.

As to the diffusion of the patterns of social roles, or their spread from community to community and from society to society, there are various well-known ways by which this process goes on: borrowing from neighboring cultures, travel, trade, migration, colonization, conquest, dissemination of book lore. But not all the similarities of roles found in different communities or societies can be thus accounted for; in many cases we must admit independent evolution along similar lines. The world-wide similarity of the roles of warrior, priest, and small agriculturalist must be explained in all probability by a combination of diffusion and parallel evolution.

The conception of social roles here outlined furnishes the background for our present problems in the "so-

SOCIOLOGY AND KNOWLEDGE

ciology of knowledge." First of all, we presume hypothetically that individuals who specialize in cultivating knowledge and are therefore called "scientists" perform social roles of a definite class. This means that there must be social circles to whom knowledge in general or systematic knowledge in particular appears to be positively valuable. Participants in these circles must be convinced that they need the coöperation of "scientists" to realize certain tendencies connected with this valuable knowledge. In order to be qualified as a scientist whom his circle needs, a person must be regarded as a "self" endowed with certain desirable characteristics and lacking certain undesirable characteristics. Social status must be granted to a person who is thus needed and qualified as a scientist. And this person must perform social functions which will satisfy the needs of his circle in the matter of knowledge; in other words, he must cultivate knowledge for the benefit of those who grant him social status.

Are there indeed such social roles? If so, what is their essential composition and structure? Are there any specific varieties among them? How are they as a class related logically to other classes of social role? And since in the social just as in the biological field genetic relationships between classes throw some light upon their logical relationships, we may ask: What is the origin of scientists' roles in general, and how did specific variations of those roles evolve? [9]

This gives us our first set of problems. They are of the

[9] Cf. F. Znaniecki, *The Method of Sociology*, Chap. VI, "Analytic Induction."

same kind as all problems of systematic description and classification of social phenomena. But because this is a study in the "sociology of knowledge," there are other borderland problems which we have to face. Are there any relationships of functional dependence between the social roles which scientists perform and the kind of knowledge which they cultivate? More specifically: Are the systems of knowledge which scientists build and their methods of building them influenced by the social patterns with which scientists are expected to conform as participants in a certain social order and by the ways in which they actually realize those patterns?

CHAPTER TWO

TECHNOLOGISTS AND SAGES

1. KNOWLEDGE A PREREQUISITE FOR ALL SOCIAL ROLES

How can it be that scientists, men who indulge in cultivating knowledge instead of being efficiently active like everybody else, are not only tolerated by men of action but granted a social status and regarded as performing a desirable social function by the communities in which they live?

This is not a rhetorical question. Scientists have been complaining for thousands of years about the little appreciation given by the mass of humankind to the knowledge they are pursuing; and sociological observers of social life agree as to how justified these complaints are. Studies of communities on lower cultural levels and of large classes of people who are actively pursuing practical occupations in more civilized societies—agriculturalists, artisans, merchants, housewives, and so on—show how relatively seldom in the normal course of their lives men of action feel any real need for those who specialize in knowledge. And even then, the question may be raised, when is the demand for the scientist's knowledge spontaneous and when is it due to the influence of certain cultural traditions?

The fact is that every individual who performs any social role is supposed by his social circle to possess and believes himself to possess the knowledge indispensable for its normal performance. If he lacks this knowledge, he is regarded as psychologically unfit for that role. Acquisition of this necessary knowledge is a part, often the main part, of the preparation which may be generally termed the "educational process"; and until the knowledge (as well as other personal characteristics required by the role) has been presumably acquired the individual is only a candidate for the role for which he is preparing. And, originally, educational processes occur under the guidance of those people who are already performing the kind of role for which candidates are being prepared. The origin and development of specific roles of "teachers" whose function is to impart knowledge to candidates for other roles than their own will be dealt with in our next chapter. Of course, not all the individuals who perform similar roles in a given community are expected or believed to possess equal knowledge; nor are they supposed to be equal in other personal characteristics required by their roles. Recognized personal inequalities lead to secondary differentiation in status and function among the persons performing roles of a certain class. Thus persons whose knowledge is regarded as inferior, like persons of inferior skill, health, initiative, or perseverance, will not be entrusted with as important tasks as persons of superior ability. But so long as a community includes persons whose knowledge is considered adequate for the performance of the various

TECHNOLOGISTS AND SAGES

practical functions which the community needs, scientists specializing in the cultivation of knowledge will not be in demand.

Such is the condition usually prevailing in comparatively simple, relatively isolated and conservative communities: preliterate peoples, rural and small-town aggregations which, though belonging to large national or political societies, take little share in their superior culture. Two kinds of knowledge are to be found in such a community: specialized knowledge which particular individuals need in their occupational roles and common knowledge which all adult individuals need as members of the community.

2. ACTIVE SPECIALISTS AND TECHNICAL KNOWLEDGE

We call the first kind of knowledge technical because it is the background and condition for a successful application of the skill required for the performance of occupational functions. A hunter is supposed to know everything necessary to catch game, everything concerning the wild animals, the implements used in hunting, and the natural factors (including magical forces) which may affect his activity. An Indian woman's domestic skills presuppose a considerable complex of information about the plants she collects, the properties of the materials and instruments used in cooking, sewing, spinning, weaving, pottery, tent-making, and so on. A farmer is expected to have all the knowledge he needs from day to day and from season to season concerning the plants he cultivates and the weeds that interfere with their cultivation, the soil and the ways of fertilizing it, the weather, horses and cattle, the various implements he uses.

This technical knowledge has a distinctly pragmatic character. The test of its validity is its practical application. But this does not mean that each particular or general "truth" included in it is separately tested in practice by a process similar to scientific experimentation or that the "truths" which stand the test remain while those that do not are rejected. It is the total personal knowledge of the hunter, the woman, the medicine man, the farmer, or at least his total knowledge concerning that portion of reality which he tries to control practically, that is subjected to the pragmatic test and approved or disapproved, depending on his final success or failure.

Every practical application of technical knowledge made by a person who is acting an occupational role occurs in a concrete situation in which many diverse objects and processes are involved. The hunter who goes on an expedition, the woman who weaves a blanket, the medicine man who treats a sick person, the farmer who raises a crop, the builder who constructs a house, the war chief who leads his troop to battle—each performs an action whose component elements, as well as the connections between them, are not only highly complex but continually changing, partly in consequence of his own activity, partly under the influence of outside factors. At the beginning of this action, he defines the situation he

TECHNOLOGISTS AND SAGES

is facing in accordance with a certain pattern he has learned to apply.

In occupational patterns, such a definition involves setting a purpose, defining in advance the result to be achieved in the future (game of a certain species to be killed, a house of a chosen size and style to be built, health to be regained by a sick person) and surveying the data in present reality which in their various relationships appear as positively or negatively significant conditions of the realization of the purpose (probable location and habits of the game, weather conditions, disposable hunting implements; the site of the future house, the nature, sources, and prices of building materials, available labor, funds at the builder's disposal; organism of the patient, the nature and cause of his sickness, his environment, accessible supply of medicines, and so on).

The definition of the situation raises the practical problem of how to achieve the purpose under the given conditions. This problem is solved by selecting and using some of the data as materials and instruments in accordance with certain methods of technical skill. Unless the whole process of solving the practical problem is exactly determined in advance and the execution perfectly skillful, formerly unnoticed or unforeseen data are bound to appear within the range of the activity; then the original situation has to be redefined and the practical problem becomes more or less different from what it was at first. This may happen a number of times before the final result is reached. Therefore, however satisfactory the result may be, it is never identical with the original purpose unless the whole action is an exact reproduction of former actions under artificially isolated and regulated conditions, as, for example, the production of the thousandth automobile of the same type in the same factory.

We see that at the first stage of an occupational performance and at several later stages the agent has to apply a considerable variety of specific information concerning the data which enter into the situation as originally defined and as later redefined and also concerning the anticipated effects of the various instrumental processes which have to be combined in order to achieve the purpose. This miscellaneous information is, of course, not chaotic; for the occupational pattern determines what set of knowledge should be used by a hunter, a medicine man, a war chief, a farmer, or a builder in performing the kinds of action which normally belong to his occupational function. But before the development of scientific technology there can be no objective reason for including or not including any separate "truth" within this set of knowledge; for the latter is not theoretically systematized apart from the personality of the agent but practically organized by him for the active performance of his function. The success of some particular action of his is regarded as a sign that he personally knew all that was necessary for him to know in order to achieve success and that he made the proper use of that knowledge at the proper time in the course of his action; failure means either that he lacked part of the necessary knowledge or did not apply it as he ought to have done. Furthermore, in the judgment of others his technical knowledge is seldom separated from his practical skill, his initiative, his persistence, his good will. To determine what part each of these "personality traits" plays in the total success or failure of his occupational activity requires a degree of reflection which is difficult at the level of cultural development we are considering here. And much more difficult, if not almost impossible at this level, would be the kind of analysis of his performances which would judge the objective validity of a certain idea of his concerning the data he deals with or the effects of the instrumental processes he uses by determining the practical consequences of the application of this idea.

It does happen, indeed, that in comparing a successful with an unsuccessful action of the same agent or of two agents in the same occupation, the difference is explicitly traced to the conflict of certain ideas which have been applied in the two cases; and occasionally this process results in an improvement of technical knowledge. But the uncertainty of this kind of test as a factor in the progress of efficiency is well demonstrated by the persistence of magical beliefs in practical occupations through centuries and millenniums. Even now there are innumerable communities which have not yet been penetrated by the rationalism of modern technology and where it is by no means rare to find the failure of an occupational performance ascribed to the agent's ignorance or disapproval of certain magical or religious forces, with the consequent omission of rites intended to influence those forces. And even apart from magic, various obviously absurd ideas have been perpetuated in some occupations—as in peasant farming and animal husbandry throughout the world—and are defended against criticism by the pragmatic argument that they have been empirically proved to "work" in practice.

Of course, the technical knowledge of particular individuals does increase and improve in practical usefulness during the period of educational preparation for specific occupational roles, and even after that period in the customary pursuit of occupational activities. But the point is that the limit of advance in every community is fixed by the personal knowledge of the particular person or of those few persons who are regarded as the most successful and therefore the most "knowing" among all who perform these specific roles. They constitute the supreme authorities in their occupation, unless perhaps there is somebody in another community whose fame for occupational efficiency and wisdom is still greater. But such technical authorities are not scientists, for it is not their knowledge as such that is in demand but their superior skill in their own occupational field, their knowledge being only an auxiliary though indispensable prerequisite. When a beginning medicine man subordinates himself to the guidance of a famous authority, when an inexperienced housewife tries to learn the methods of a woman who has earned general admiration for the products of her domestic activities, when a young medieval artisan travels halfway across Europe to work and study under a renowned master of his craft, what is sought is not theory but a model for practical imitation.

No demand for a scientist as a bearer of superior knowledge can arise among the persons engaged in a practical occupation so long as those persons are convinced that any situation which appears in the performance of their roles can be fitted into some general pattern with which the best, if not all, of them are familiar. And in the absence of scientists, the craft is the only judge of its own knowledge and skill. It sets the standards of technical success; it has well-tried methods of meeting the criticism of outsiders by explaining failures away; if an individual failure has to be admitted, it will be presumably redeemed by future successes of the same person or of better persons within the craft.

3. THE OCCUPATIONAL ADVISER AND THE BEGINNINGS OF TECHNOLOGICAL KNOWLEDGE

Difficulties appear only when the persons performing certain functions become aware that they are facing a kind of situation which they do not know how to define because it does not fit into any familiar pattern. This awareness may come in two ways. Either the conditions under which occupational functions are performed undergo unexpectedly an important change, or else new ways of defining situations with new standards of success and failure in solving practical problems are introduced into the community in consequence of cultural contacts with other communities or individual innovation.

The first source of disturbance may be exemplified by the appearance of a sickness with unfamiliar symptoms, an unexpected scarcity of game or fish, an unknown pest ravaging the crops, difficulty in getting material or instruments hitherto used in handiwork, invasion by enemies armed with unfamiliar weapons, new taxes or other burdens laid upon a community by the state. Examples of the second source of disturbance are: new kinds of goods brought by foreign merchants and displacing local products in the popular demand; a new handicraft introduced by immigrants or returning travelers; new methods of curing sickness, of cultivating or fertilizing land, of craftsmanship, of housekeeping (imitated from abroad or slowly evolving through personal initiative); importation of new varieties of grain or of domestic animals; discovery of unexploited mineral resources which are in demand outside of the community.

Under such circumstances, doubts are apt to arise even among the best occupational authorities as to the proper ways of defining such unfamiliar situations and solving the new practical problems which they involve. Eventually, they come to realize the inadequacy of their technical knowledge and to seek enlightenment from someone with superior knowledge. The alternative—to confess the inefficiency of their practical skill—is both objectively and subjectively unsatisfactory. For their difficulty is that they do not know what ought to be done: once they learn this, they presume that they will be able to do it. And we find that confession of ignorance comes apparently much more easily to practical people and seems less humiliating than confession of incapacity. This is not surprising in view of the fact that their social circles need and expect from them chiefly technical skill and are much less interested in the technical knowledge underlying that skill.

Thus we find in communities where unexpected changes disturb established occupational patterns a demand for advisers whom people actively performing occupational roles can consult when in doubt. Because it is not the skill of the practical people, but their knowledge, which is in question, knowledge and not skill is sought in an adviser. It is preferable—nay, often essential—that he should not be active in a practical role of the same kind as that of those who consult him: he must be beyond competition, so that men of action may be sure his advice is disinterested. In case of disagreement they will then defer to his judgment and subject their opinions to his arbitration.

We find two early varieties of advisers. One is the priest. His main function is, of course, practical: he is supposed to control magical forces directly and to influence religious powers on behalf of the community and its members. But in addition he is often consulted by people who in their occupational roles meet unexpectedly with critical incomprehensible situations. Especially on lower stages of technical evolution, in difficult or dangerous natural conditions, this is a frequent occurrence; life is full of what Sumner (*Folkways*) calls "the aleatory element"—imprevisible accidents which existing technical knowledge cannot explain. And here is where the priest's mysterious knowledge of things hidden from other people comes in. While in important events, especially those affecting whole groups, he may be asked to act himself in accordance with his religious function, in many cases all that is expected of him is to supply the knowledge which others lack to solve their own difficulties. He explains the essence and origin of facts which befall the hunter, the warrior, the sailor, the husbandman, and which they do not understand; he interprets mysterious signs of gods and foretells the future; he advises people what gods to address and what methods to use for their propitiation.[1]

This function of the priest, however, though it was very important in the past and persists even now in simpler conservative communities, has not given birth to so significant developments as that of the lay adviser; and its value has greatly diminished with the advance of technology. On the one hand, the priest's advice is difficult to test pragmatically, in so far as it is based upon sacred knowledge about things beyond the experience of laymen. We shall return to this matter in discussing the sacred lore of priestly scholars. On the other hand, the priest, having his own practical occupational role to perform, cannot possess all the special knowledge which men in any other occupational role—hunters, farmers, artisans—may need in an emergency; he can advise only about the magical and religious factors that enter into unusual situations and not about other elements of those

---

[1] This intellectual leadership of the priest in matters of technological knowledge has been emphasized by Frazer.

situations. Of course, priests may acquire special knowledge of a predominantly secular character connected with occupations that are not essentially religious: medicine in Egypt, Babylonia, and Greece is an instance. But if he gives people in occupational roles advice founded on this kind of knowledge, his function does not differ much from that of a lay adviser.

The latter is primarily an old person who has retired from the active life during which he was a prominent authority in his field. Sometimes he is a widely traveled man who, like Odysseus, "saw the cities of many men and knew their minds" but was perhaps less absorbed in his own troubles than Odysseus. Occasionally he is a foreign visitor who is not expected to compete with local people. Or he may be a man whom his status raises above competition, like the owner of a large estate in a peasant community, if the peasants trust him personally. But in any case, to be asked for advice, particularly to be referred to as an arbiter between diverging opinions of practical authorities, such a person must presumably have a much broader knowledge than those who consult him. His knowledge should not be limited, like theirs, to personal occupational experience, however long and successful, but should include a considerable range of trustworthy *observation* of other people's occupational activities in various roles.

This means that he is expected to know not merely how to deal practically with a specific kind of technical problem but what are the different ways in which various kinds of people define the situations they meet in the course of their occupational activities; he is supposed to have observed diverse instruments and methods used to solve practical problems not only in one occupation but in several connected occupations, not only in one community but in various communities. In other words, not only the values used and created by technical actions but the technical actions themselves are meant to constitute the object matter of his knowledge; he is not a man who practices a technique but a man who studies techniques. Such knowledge as his is termed *technological*.

When an adviser is consulted about a doubtful situation, the original technical problem in which the acting person's knowledge and skill are inseparably involved becomes subdivided into a theoretic and a practical part. The arbiter's task is first of all theoretic—a task of *diagnosis*. He has to define the data of the situation, discover its essential components and their connections, as well as find out how it originated. Something is happening in nature, in human organic life, or in cultural life which men active in occupational roles do not understand; the adviser with his superior and broader knowledge solves for them this theoretic problem.

The practical problem remains to be solved: how to attain the given purpose under the conditions thus diagnosed by instrumentally modifying reality. However, before the action reaches the instrumental stage there must be a reflective determination of the result to be aimed at and a mental choice and organization of those processes by which this result will be most satisfactorily achieved. In an ordinary situation which people performing occupational roles define and deal with by their own capacities, all this is easy: the determination of the purpose is included in the definition of the situation, and settled rules dictate how to handle this kind of situation.

But in an unusual situation which only a person with technological knowledge can understand, the purpose must be adapted to unfamiliar conditions; and instead of a habitual application of customary technical rules, a more or less new way of acting has to be devised in advance so as to foresee and overcome obstacles to successful achievement. After the theoretic problem of diagnosis has been solved, two tasks remain to be performed: *making a plan,* which is a problem of applied knowledge, and *executing* or *realizing the plan,* which is a problem of technical skill.

And here the man with technological knowledge is faced by important alternatives. He may, after making the diagnosis, form the plan for men of action to follow; this means that he takes upon himself the responsibility for the consequences and thus subjects the knowledge upon which the plan was based to the pragmatic test—provided, of course, the men of action do not bungle. Or else he may not commit himself to any practical consequences of his diagnosis and the final responsibility for making and executing the plan may remain with the men of action.

In the early role of adviser who gives his opinion when consulted by active performers of occupational roles, in any particular case it depends partly on what they want, partly on his own will, whether this opinion will contain a diagnosis and a plan or merely a diagnosis. Eventually, however, either the one or the other may come to be regularly expected by a social circle which centers around the person possessing technological knowledge. As we pass from relatively small and simple communities to societies of greater size and complexity, we find two different kinds of technological role: the *technological leader* defines situations and makes plans for technicians to execute; the *technological expert* specializes in diagnosis. And when these roles become finally stabilized, individuals explicitly prepare for them.

4. TECHNOLOGICAL LEADERS

When an occupational task requires the coöperation of a number of people, there is a technical leader who coördinates their activities, unless this coördination, through frequent repetition, has become a matter of routine. If the task is such that technological knowledge is deemed necessary for its performance, the technical leader is expected to possess this knowledge, to be a technological leader who will diagnose the situation and make the plan for his followers to execute under his technical guidance. In simple and stable societies, when a new and difficult situation necessitates collective action, it often happens that an adviser who has retired from active life is asked to assume this kind of leadership and not only to make a plan for others but to direct its execution. In more complex and changing societies, where the need of technological knowledge in technical lead-

TECHNOLOGISTS AND SAGES

ers is more or less clearly recognized, individuals destined to lead others in collective performances prepare in advance by acquiring the technological knowledge that will be expected of them, learning to use it in making diagnoses and plans. Thus the preparation of the future leader in warfare includes comparative knowledge of military tactics and strategy as well as of weapons, fortifications, siege implements, and so on; the future builder of roads and bridges, the constructor of ports or of irrigation systems, the architect, the shipbuilder or navigator must not merely be trained in technical skill but foresee the various technical situations which the group that he will lead may have to face—often unexpectedly. He knows how to determine in advance, often in considerable detail, the result which this group will be made to achieve under his guidance, as well as the distribution among its members of the various instrumental processes which must be combined for the realization of this result.

As in modern times collective tasks take to a growing degree the place of individual tasks in almost every field of technical endeavor, the roles of technological leaders multiply and specialize and their knowledge becomes more and more thorough and precise. Not only have they become indispensable in industry, but even in such domains of human activity as commerce, banking, and finance, where the data of practical situations include, besides material objects, conscious human beings, many occupational functions are carried on by groups of diversified specialists under the leadership of men who in order to perform their roles have purposely acquired a vast complex of technological knowledge. Moreover, the technological leader seldom directs personally the actual instrumental processes by which the final result is achieved but, having planned those processes and their distribution, leaves a subordinate technical leader to supervise the execution of his plan. Finally, in large groups with intricate tasks the very functions of diagnosis and planning become subdivided: deliberative committees diagnose broadly and synthetically the entire complex of various situations which the group is facing or expected to face presently and indicate the general direction of its activities; a technological leader together with a staff of assistant leaders diagnoses more exactly each specific type of situation and draws a total plan, including a number of diverse and specific plans the execution of which will be left to subgroups of specialized technicians.

The technological leader must obviously be a "scientist," a man of knowledge whose function is to cultivate and use this knowledge for the benefit of those who lack it and need it in their occupational roles. But he is also a social leader, the head of a group whose activities he directs. And his social leadership overshadows and conditions his functions as a scientist, for it gives him institutional power within the group, and in so far as he controls the collective forces of the latter it becomes a source of social prestige and influence in the wider society of which this group forms a part. There are various ways in which he can attain this status: he may inherit it, or be elected to it by the group, or climb to it from subordinate positions within the group, or be appointed to it by a leader of a superior dominant group, or take it by force because he has the support of some socially powerful group. But he can maintain it only by avoiding such mistakes in his technological planning as will result in the failure of the group to achieve its purposes.

Failure has much more serious consequences in the case of a group specially organized for technical tasks than in the case of an individual technician working alone, because of the relative magnitude of the tasks, the losses which their nonfulfillment involves, and the disorganizing influence which it has upon the group. The leader is made responsible for those consequences, with the effect that his social status is lowered in the eyes of the group and of the wider social milieu. And whereas in the case of a religious or political leader such an effect can be counteracted by a strikingly successful achievement, a technological leader is less fortunate in this respect. For under technological planning, what is regarded as normal success is accepted as a matter of course, while the plan—if strictly followed—seldom leaves any opportunity for unexpected, extraordinary success. Consequently, it is more important for the technological leader not to fall below the standard of expected achievement than to rise above it.

Though the technological leader is also a social leader, yet the test of success and failure is considered primarily a test of his knowledge and only secondarily of his capacity for social leadership, since the members of a group selected and organized for technical achievement are supposed to be willing and technically able to do what he wants them to do, while his own technical skill does not come under consideration at all. Thus his knowledge, though still personal like that of the technician, is separated from his other personal characteristics, and its composition and structure are directly dependent on his social role.

First of all, it is supposed to be *certain* knowledge. Only proven truths should be included in it; there is no place in it for hypotheses that need further testing, since the possibility of error means the possibility of failure in group action. At the same time, it must be *inductive* knowledge, based on generalization from individual empirical data. How can the certainty of proven truth be attached to an inductive generalization? By limiting its extension to the range of data within which it has been already tested; in practice, this means refraining from its application to data which seem different from those to which it has already been applied. The technological leader has to be suspicious of new data. Suppose, for instance, he has previous knowledge based on experience and observation about the characteristics of a specific kind of technical material—wood, stone, metal—which has proved useful for the kind of task his group is undertaking. He is expected to be suspicious if offered material which seems to possess somewhat different characteristics, and his suspicion can be allayed only by a series of tests which will show that the difference is irrelevant to the kind of use to which this material is to be put. Of course he is not concerned with the strictly logical distinction between certainty and high probability; a generalization is certain to him if no exceptions have yet been found in the course of technological observation. When, as often in modern times, he takes his inductive generalizations from theoretic research he is careful to select only those which do not at the time give rise to any new theoretic problems.

Furthermore, the technological leader's knowledge must be of the kind which makes prediction possible, in accordance with Auguste Comte's famous formula: "Savoir pour prévoir, prévoir pour pouvoir." This means that he must know the causal relations between processes of change. He ought to be able to predict that if, for example, to a certain material certain instruments are applied in agreement with a certain technical method, definite changes will occur in the material. But causal relations are predictable only if the processes of cause and effect are repeatable; and these are repeatable only if the conditions under which they occur are similar at each occurrence. Of course, for practical purposes, approximate repetition of processes and approximate similarity of the conditions are sufficient (though the more precise and detailed the plan of the action, the closer must be this approximation). Nonetheless the technological leader is faced by a fundamental difficulty. For his guidance is required only when the situation in which technical activity has to proceed is comparatively new, and this implies that the conditions under which a causal connection between processes is supposed to be realized are not similar to those under which it was realized in the past. Either the technical process which used to be the cause of certain changes cannot be reproduced under the new conditions or its effect is bound to be interfered with by other causal factors. What the technological leader must do if he wants the causally related processes to be repeated is to reproduce artificially the conditions under which they have been known to occur, by either introducing into the changed conditions whatever is needed to realize the cause, or counteracting whatever interferes with the realization of the effect, or both. This must be done for every causal connection which is a necessary means for the realization of the end. It presupposes the performance of various preparatory and auxiliary actions each of which requires some knowledge of causal relations not included in the usual technical performance.

Consequently, the total personal knowledge of the technological leader cannot be reduced to any system of theoretic special "truths" bearing upon an abstractly isolated section of reality. It must be a set of heterogeneous knowledge [2] organized entirely with reference to the collective tasks the achievement of which he plans and directs. The nucleus of this knowledge is constituted by those "truths" which he directly applies in all his plans. The civil engineer who builds bridges must have the necessary physical and chemical knowledge involved in planning the construction of any bridge under whatever conditions. For vast portions of physics and chemistry,

---

[2] We find this requirement exemplified in the biographies of such American "captains of industry" as Andrew Carnegie, John D. Rockefeller, J. Pierpont Morgan.

however, he will have no use except under conditions so improbable that for practical purposes their possibility may be neglected. But he must have some knowledge of geology, geography, and meteorology to take into account various natural conditions under which bridges have to be built; and he should know something of economics, sociology, and psychology to utilize favorable and counteract unfavorable factors which have their source in the cultural life of men. All this miscellaneous peripheral knowledge, though less precise than that which goes into his plan of the bridge, ought to be of the kind that will enable him to subsume the data he meets under classes already well defined and to predict with practically sufficient probability what will be the effects of changes which occur without his interference or through his agency.

In short, in every diagnosis the technological leader is supposed to reduce whatever is new and uncertain in the complex situation he is facing to a practically safe combination of old and certain truths about things and processes.

As a matter of fact, however, there are and have been for many centuries technological leaders who go beyond the requirements and expectations of their social milieu, who by their own initiative, not in response to a social demand, undertake new collective tasks involving considerable risks, inasmuch as there is no sufficiently secure basis for their plans in preëxisting knowledge. Such leaders must be men of great power or prestige enabling them to form groups for the realization of those tasks and to maintain their social roles in case their first attempts fail. In the main, they have been either rulers of states or, oftener still, persons to whom rulers delegate their power for specific technical aims. To them is due much of the progress achieved since the times of ancient Egypt and Babylonia in architecture, military and civil engineering, mining, navigation. In recent times, while the most important and novel undertakings in those fields are still mainly due to state initiative, in the domain of collective industrial production the boldest of the collective technological tasks are carried on with the support of economic power wielded by "captains of industry."

A planned collective task for which no complete and certain theoretic foundation exists may be achieved in two ways. In the first way, the technological leader uses untested hypotheses in planning and changes his plans as soon as he finds by trial that these hypotheses "do not work," that their practical application has unexpected results. This is, of course, a costly method in a collective undertaking, and the final result of the latter is bound to be different from what was originally intended. Still, this does not necessarily mean that it must always be worthless when judged not by the standard of conformity between achievement and purpose but by some extraneous standards of utility; it may prove as valuable as the intended result would have been, or even more valuable. Then it is regarded as a success. The other way is to ascertain the validity of untested hypotheses by observation or experiment before the plan is carried into execution, modifying it if necessary to diminish the risk. The technological leader may perform this function himself; if, however, he is primarily a social leader, a man of power to whom the acquisition of knowledge is a mere instrument for the control of group activities, or if this task is too vast and complicated for him to acquire all the knowledge needed for its performance, he entrusts this function to a subordinate specialist—an expert.

5. TECHNOLOGICAL EXPERTS

In the social role of the technological expert, knowledge is completely separated from its practical applications. Not only has he no share in the ultimate performance either as a technical worker or as a technical leader of workers, but he has no responsibility for deciding what technical activities are to be performed. The decision belongs to the technological leader, and all the expert has to do is to furnish whatever special knowledge the leader lacks and needs before he decides. The character and the amount of knowledge that is demanded of him is relative to what the leader himself is socially supposed to know and believes he knows; but in any case the leader alone determines what use he will make of the expert's knowledge to supplement his own. It often happens, indeed, that experts are entrusted by leaders with the task of planning at least in part the collective achievement to come; this means that they are more than experts and that they share—even if unofficially—in the function of leadership.

Kings, war lords, high priests, administrators, judges, legislators, and economic entrepreneurs have been using experts for many centuries not to advise them what they ought to do but to gather and make available to them reliable knowledge about some specific and as yet insufficiently known data pertaining to the total practical situation or about the effects of some new processes anticipated but untried. There have been astrologers, geomants, augurs, and state experts in demography, public health, meteorology, geography, geology, agriculture, mining, industry, and finance. In modern warfare, military staffs are employing experts, specialists drawn from nearly every field of scientific knowledge. Naturally, when a group leader has but little technological knowledge (as is usually the case with political leaders who have not been prepared for technological leadership in any field but only for social leadership) almost all the information needed for any collective task must be gathered by experts. But it is the leader, the man in power (or the group in power), who imposes upon experts the theoretic problems to be solved. Even when experts take the initiative in investigating facts and communicating the results of their research to the men in power, they select such problems as will presumably interest the latter.

This sets definite limitations on their research. The results of the latter must be known in advance to be relevant to the practical task contemplated by the leader, whether it be filling the state treasury, combating epidemics, raising the level of agriculture, planning a war,

TECHNOLOGISTS AND SAGES

building a railroad, or producing faster airplanes. The facts to be studied are already defined, and it is supposed that they have a certain bearing, desirable or undesirable from the leader's point of view, upon the present situation or will have a certain influence upon the results of the activities which are being planned. The problem is to test the first kind of supposition by observation, the second kind by experiment, and to find whether it can be relied upon or, if there are alternative suppositions, which of the two can be relied upon. Concerning the facts in question, no new hypotheses are wanted which are not relevant to their practical significance for the task contemplated; and new problems are definitely unwanted.

This advance determination of the kind of knowledge that is demanded from an expert is most obvious in the role of statistical expert. In simple enumeration, the nature of each of the data to be enumerated is presumed to be known, for only those characters of the data are taken into account in their definition which have already been found to be practically significant; what the expert has to discover is the frequency distribution of those data within the range of the leader's activity (for example, the frequency distribution of various-sized incomes within the limits of the state) in so far as this has a bearing upon the actual practical situation (for example, replenishing the treasury). When a statistical correlation is sought, there is an assumption that data of one series are often causally dependent upon data of the other series; and the expert is to find out whether this dependence is sufficiently frequent to justify an attempt to influence quantitatively the first series by modifying quantitatively the second, for instance, to check crime, pauperism, or prostitution by prohibiting the sale of alcoholic drinks or to improve the crops in the country by popularizing the use of artificial fertilizers. Furthermore, when the task of the expert is to obtain knowledge pertaining to the actual situation, his field is circumscribed in space and time; he has to study facts that are important here and now, without seeking by comparative methods to reach generalizations that will be valid irrespective of actual conditions.

It is different, however, if the expert's task involves technological *experimentation*. The latter consists in testing, on a small scale or in a few cases, the results of actions which are to be performed on a large scale or in a great many cases. Here also the expert's problem is originally limited, for he is to find out whether and under what conditions a certain kind of action will have the kind of result that has been anticipated in the tentative formation of the leader's plan. Thus the medical expert, applying experimentally to a number of animal organisms a certain hygienic measure intended to prevent infection by an epidemic disease, tests the hypothesis that the spread of this disease among the population of the country will be prevented if the state authorities apply this measure to all the inhabitants. An agricultural expert in an experiment station tries crop rotation or the use of a fertilizer in order to discover whether this kind of action, if generalized among the farmers, will

TECHNOLOGISTS AND SAGES

raise the productivity of their farms. The chemical expert applies in the laboratory a certain dye to certain textiles and exposes the textiles thus dyed to the influence of sunlight, water, and so on, so as to test in advance the results anticipated from the use of this dye in mass production. This kind of experimental task presupposes that the causal processes which the expert uses are already known and that their effects have been hypothetically induced from previous experience, but that the hypotheses lack the degree of certainty or precision that is required for successful planning. The expert does not initiate any new knowledge; he only perfects existing knowledge.

But the task of the expert may go further. If he finds that the kind of action which was planned will fail to produce the desired result, he may be asked to devise a more successful kind of action; or if he discovers by experimentation that an unforeseen factor will interfere with the achievement of the leader's purpose, he may be expected to find a way of counteracting this factor. In a word, his social function may include attempts to *invent alternative patterns* of technical actions more effective for the achievement of the final purpose than those foreseen in the tentative plan of the leader. Sometimes still greater ingenuity is expected of him. The technological leader may lack even hypothetical knowledge as to the possible ways in which a certain specific and partial result essential for the realization of his final purpose can be brought about. Without such knowledge his plan is not merely tentative: it is necessarily incomplete. The expert may be then required to invent some way yet unknown of completing and effectively realizing the leader's plan. To do it, he must successively try various combinations of hypotheses, old and new, and test them experimentally in application to his particular problem, until he has found a combination that "works," that is, until he has invented a pattern of technical action which is sure to produce the desired result.

We speak of inventing a new pattern of technical action, not a new technical object or process. The common conception of an "invention" as used in popular thinking, in legal norms (for example, those which regulate the granting of patents), and even in theoretic reflection arbitrarily isolates objects or processes from the total active technical systems of which they are elements and within which only they have a practical meaning.[3] Such an approach makes impossible a comparative scientific analysis of inventions as dynamic cultural phenomena and will have to be discarded, just as modern ethnologists are discarding the method of collecting and classifying the technical implements of lower peoples in ethnographical museums without reference to the problem of how such implements are connected in active usage with other cultural values of those peoples.

The fact is that every object or process that is invented

[3] This kind of approach is necessarily used in statistical studies of the numerical growth and spread of "inventions." We do not mean to disparage such studies; only it must be clearly understood that they are dealing not with inventions as cultural phenomena but only with those products of technical activity which are regarded and accepted as new technical values in a certain collectivity.

TECHNOLOGISTS AND SAGES

is a technical value which must be viewed in connection with two dynamic, active systems. On the one hand, it is a product of the inventor's original technical action in which he has selected and used in a new way, as materials, instruments, and standardized processes, certain values which were already in existence, thus giving them a new practical meaning (which may be manifested, for instance, in a growing social demand for those values, if the invention spreads). In the course of this action, the materials, instruments, processes have to be modified in adaptation to the new value the inventor intends to produce, and the latter must be gradually modified in adaptation to them. In order to produce other values of the same kind as the inventor first produces, technicians will have to "imitate" his original action, to apply the active pattern he invented, though eventually this pattern will be improved, made more effective by secondary inventive modifications.

On the other hand, if the new value is used (and so long as it remains unused it has no practical meaning outside of the inventor's original action), it becomes incorporated into some other dynamic system, is selected by somebody as an element of another action. The latter may be also technical, as when a new building material is used to construct a house, a new agricultural implement to cultivate a field, a new chemical process to dye textiles. But it may be some other kind of action: a new food product to be eaten, a new type of clothes to be worn; while an automobile may serve as an instrument in different kinds of action ranging from churchgoing to robbery, from saving human lives by medicine and surgery to taking human lives in war.

And an action which uses a new product of invention cannot exactly follow an old pattern: it must deviate from it, in however slight a degree, and be thus in some measure inventive, for other values included in it have to be adapted to the new value. This adaptation may vary within wide limits. For example, while little innovation may be needed in a pattern of food consumption to introduce a new kind of preserved food, in order to use cement instead of brick or stone in building a house, new instruments have to be devised to handle it; technical processes have to be changed; and the house itself as a product has to be differently planned. The change from man-driven tools to steam-driven machines in any industry has been made possible only by important modifications of traditional action patterns and sometimes even an introduction of unprecedented patterns. The wide and manifold use of the automobile implies such important and diverse patterns of social and economic actions on which community life was founded as to revolutionize the whole traditional structure of the community.

Coming back now to the social function of the technological expert, we find that when an invention is expected of him his problem is determined by the use to which the technological leader plans to put the product of his inventive action. This product is defined in advance as a necessary "means" for the realization of the leader's "end"; and because the leader has a definite

TECHNOLOGISTS AND SAGES

situation to cope with and knows what kind of end he wants to attain, the expert's invention ought to just fill the need and not require for its use any further important innovations on the leader's part.

Thus, an industrial leader using experts to invent the most effective way of producing a certain kind of commodity for which he is sure to find a market does not welcome an invention which cannot be utilized except by scrapping all the machinery in his factory and ordering new machinery; or which, instead of the commodity he intends to produce, shows how to manufacture an unknown commodity which cannot be marketed except at great risk and expense. When modern "captains of industry" who maintain laboratories for technological experimentation shelve inventions of their experts that are too original and important to be used without disturbing the technical or economic structure of their enterprises and keep them secret lest bolder competitors use them, they act in perfect accordance with the traditional dependence of the expert's function upon the demands of the technological leader.

6. INDEPENDENT INVENTORS

Inventive technological experimentation, however, is not exclusively or even predominantly carried on by experts working to satisfy the requirements of leaders. For many centuries it has been freely indulged in by individuals performing various occupational roles but spending much of their energy in search for untried technical ways, by leaders who have used their leisure time to test new possibilities of anticipated future leadership, by experts who have gone beyond their regular function as determined by the actual needs of their leaders and tried to invent new technical action patterns in the hope that a demand for them would eventually arise, and even by wealthy amateurs.[4] History lists names of numerous inventors from classical antiquity to recent times; we may mention, by way of example, Thales, Heron of Alexandria, Archimedes, Galen, Roger Bacon, Paracelsus, Giovanni de la Fontana, the Marquis of Winchester, James Watt, Edison. From past historical periods we get significant indirect glimpses which, coupled with direct data from the present period, allow us to conclude that the number of independent inventors little known or soon forgotten exceeds many times the sum of those who were fortunate enough to strike upon some new pattern which their wider social milieus were willing to adopt, regarding it as sufficiently important to record the initiator's name for posterity.

The striking point is that until the second half of the nineteenth century no regular social role of independent "inventor" was recognized by any social circle except among the inventors themselves, and even now such roles exist only in a few institutions for technological research. To understand this, we must remember that, although invention originates in response to a social demand, yet in all conservative societies it has been con-

[4] The influence of amateurs on invention and experimental fact-finding is well characterized by Marthe Ornstein, *The Role of Scientific Societies in the Seventeenth Century* (Chicago, 1938), pp. 54 ff.

sidered dangerous as infringing upon the existing order, be it magical, religious, social, or economic. Only if the given order is already disturbed, as in those cases where established occupational patterns cease to work, invention is justified by the need to cope with this disturbance: this is what the early adviser and later the technological leader are expected to do, since the risk they take in such a situation is necessary to counteract otherwise inevitable evils. But we have seen that even the technological leader is not supposed to take unnecessary risks; if he does, it is because he relies on his own social power or the power of a superior social leader who protects him; and when he does, he tries to diminish the risk by using experts for preliminary research and experimentation and putting them to work only upon prescribed tasks. While in a complex and changing civilization, where disturbances in various occupational fields multiply, the growth of technological leadership and of expert work lifts gradually the traditional ban on innovations in the technical domain, letting odd individuals more or less freely play with various new technical possibilities is a long way from a positive recognition of unchecked inventiveness as a socially desirable function connected with a definite social status.

We used the word "play" above intentionally, for inventors in the past seemed to have gained freedom by not being taken seriously. In the late Middle Ages and far into the seventeenth century, every invention which threatened to interfere with the important business of life—religion, politics, warfare, medicine, agriculture, commerce, handicraft—was apt to bring upon the inventor the accusation of sorcery; whereas inventions which seemed mere ingenious amusements for the idle escaped this accusation and were willingly toyed with, as is shown by the wide circulation of books describing them. Is this perhaps the reason why in China, with its conception of human life and culture as integral and influential parts of a unique and sacred world's order, so many inventions essentially similar to those which eventually revolutionized Western techniques remained mere playthings for centuries? Even in the Greco-Roman world much of the ingenuity of inventors was spent on mere toys. Heron of Alexandria in his *Pneumatica,* along with mechanical devices used in temples or in warfare, lists contrivances of a purely playful character, such as singing birds, drinking animals, marvelous vases.

Obviously, the dominant interest of the independent inventor in his field is technological, not social; he becomes absorbed in the very process of experimenting and creating new technical patterns, just as the artist becomes absorbed in his art. Independent inventors seldom specialize in any definite occupational field—unless the field is so vast as to provide unlimited new possibilities, as, for example, modern medicine, including surgery and pharmacology. He usually rambles over vast territories, recognizing no social boundaries between occupations, unhampered by the social demands for efficient technical action which would satisfy existing needs. This does not mean, however, that social considerations are absent from his life. He does want to perform a recognized

TECHNOLOGISTS AND SAGES

social role, to find or to form around him a social circle that will appreciate his personal worth; he claims a social status, including an economic position (unless this position is otherwise secured), and—most of all—he wishes to have his voluntarily assumed function socially acknowledged, his unrequired inventions used by others, his uncalled-for technological guidance followed.

Several factors determine the reception of the inventor's initiative by his social milieu. An invention which solves an original problem of the inventor and not a problem that has arisen in the course of standardized occupational activity is seldom achieved at once in a practically workable form: many auxiliary and supplementary inventions may be needed before its usefulness will be acknowledged by technicians, who apply to it the standards of efficiency of established technical patterns, or even by technological leaders concerned about achieving predetermined results of collective activity. Take such familiar examples as the history of the steam engine, the locomotive, the automobile, and the various devices for flying in the air. The vision of an inventor is needed to appreciate the possibilities of an invention which is not yet ready for practical application by technicians and also to realize what other inventions, already made or to be made, must be combined with it to make it fully useful.

The lonely inventor is a rather helpless, tragicomic figure: a few of his new devices which can be fitted into existing technical patterns may be accepted, most of his minor inventions are viewed as mere curiosities and usually forgotten after his death, while his great dreams about new ways of controlling nature are simply laughed to scorn by sober people. Only when in a society inventors multiply and learn about one another's activities by observing those results which become public, by establishing personal contacts, or through the medium of published writings, the results of past inventiveness are utilized as data for new technological creation. Incomplete or imperfect inventions are completed or perfected, inventions in different lines of technique become combined in a new synthesis, new possibilities unnoticed by one inventor are discovered and realized by others, ideas too indefinite for immediate application are gradually developed and made concrete, until what began as a toy becomes a model for the production of hitherto unknown utilities, an amusement for the idle changes into a serious occupation, a bold dream grows into an astonishing reality. Since more and more new inventions are incorporated into occupational roles, technical patterns are becoming increasingly diversified and interdependent, more and more new problems arise in the course of occupational functions. As a result, the demand for technologists grows to be more extensive and continuous, and among the technologists appear more inventors; this in turn results in a further multiplication and diversification of technically utilized inventions; and so on.

It must be remarked, however, that even the existence of many inventors in a society does not always assure this development of inventions by mutual stimulation. Many inventors have guarded the secret of their inventions from possible competitors, either fearing for their status or—in recent times—compelled to do so by powerful employers, public or private. And even if an invention is finally perfected and ready for practical uses, social forces may still resist its utilization—such social forces as the occupational conservatism of technicians who do not like to have traditional patterns discarded or modified, the opposition of those who are afraid that the adoption of the invention will impair their economic positions or interfere with the existing demand for their functions, and the passive resistance of the very people whom the invention is supposed to benefit but who do not wish their familiar ways of life disturbed by any "newfangled" devices.

In so far, however, as informal coöperation of inventors does increase, it brings a certain order into the originally disjointed knowledge which each individual inventor uses in his activity. While each particular invention represents an application of many different theoretic generalizations, old or new, and each theoretic generalization may be applied in many different inventions, when multiplying inventions cross-fertilize and supplement one another there appears a common stock of theoretic knowledge concerning a certain domain of reality which every individual inventor must share in order to participate in the growing technological control of this domain. Good examples are medicine and mechanics in classical antiquity and animal husbandry and agriculture since the eighteenth century.

Between such theoretic knowledge of technologists,

which is organized with reference to practical problems, and the theoretic knowledge of scholars and (later) of scientific explorers, which is logically organized without regard to its practical applications, a mutual influence has grown up. This is due in the main to the fact that with the development of technological education some inventors have become teachers in schools—medical, engineering, agricultural, and so on—and some teachers have become inventors; while, still more recently, institutes for scientific research have grouped together inventors and theoretic investigators. Consequently, theoretic scientists have adopted experimentation from technologists and are using it as a method of discovering and testing new truths, while technologists are assimilating logically organized systems of theoretic science and following their evolution in order to use for the purposes of invention whatever components of these systems can be so used at the given stage of technological progress.[5]

There is no doubt that the progress achieved in the technical control of natural reality during the historical period of cultural evolution, and especially during the last three centuries, is due in the main to the coöperation of technological leaders, experts, and independent inventors, that is, of those "scientists" whose function consists in cultivating the knowledge needed to make plans which technicians execute and to invent new patterns

[5] On this new relationship between the inventor and the theoretic investigator, see Fleming and Pearce, *Research in Industry* (London, 1922), pp. 151 ff.

TECHNOLOGISTS AND SAGES

which technicians imitate. Certainly, many innovations were made and still are made by skillful technicians in the course of their occupational work; but these remain within the range of possibilities that can be immediately realized by the technicians themselves and consist in perfecting plans already made or patterns already invented, rather than in making new plans or inventing new patterns—unless a technologist takes hold of such an innovation and develops it beyond its original range.

Many modern thinkers who survey and admire the progress of technology in dealing with inorganic and organic nature express surprise that no similar control of cultural, particularly social, phenomena has yet been achieved; and social scientists are frequently blamed for this failure. Even among the social scientists themselves, there are some who voice this opinion and declare that the social sciences should prove their usefulness by devising ways of influencing planfully and effectively the phenomena with which they are dealing. There seems to be, indeed, some justification in making social scientists responsible for the lack of a technology in their field which could be even distantly compared with that found in engineering or medicine, for the explanation of this fact is to be sought, we believe, in the specific variety of social roles which social scientists have performed almost exclusively in the past and which a large number of them are still performing. But these roles, like most other social roles, have originated in specific demands for socially useful knowledge which certain circles have been making on certain men and which the latter have been trying to satisfy. During the last century and a half, some scientists studying cultural phenomena have broken away from this traditional pattern and begun to develop a theoretic knowledge independent of practical social purposes, expecting that eventually a new type of technologist will apply the results of their investigation to social practice. Those people who now demand that such scientists make themselves useful by having their knowledge serve social aims and ideals probably do not realize that they demand the perpetuation of that very pattern of "social scientist" which has hitherto prevented the development of a really useful social technology.

7. COMMON-SENSE KNOWLEDGE

While the knowledge of the technologist evolves out of the technical knowledge of occupational specialists, the knowledge of the scientist who deals with cultural phenomena originates in that set of nonspecialized information about language, religion, magic, economic processes, customs, mores, persons, and groups which individuals in a given society are supposed to possess in order to perform the roles of members in this society. Of course, not everybody is expected to have equal knowledge in this general and common field: the young presumably know less than the old; the knowledge of social leaders and rulers ought to be more extensive and comprehensive than that of ordinary members. But the most essential part of it, that which is regarded as indispensable to have collective life run its regular course, must be common to all; anybody whose information

TECHNOLOGISTS AND SAGES

does not include that minimum, unless a child or a stranger, is a fool, and in any case unfit to participate in collective life. Nor can there be disagreements as to its validity: anyone who doubts any part of it is mentally or morally deranged. This is *common-sense* knowledge which concerns the supposed foundations of the existing cultural order and as such is obviously certain. For every explicit or implicit generalization which it contains is connected with some rule of cultural conduct. A knowledge of vocabulary and grammar underlies the rules of verbal communication; popular religious and magical knowledge is bound up with rites and abstentions which every individual is expected to observe in the regular course of his life; a common-sense economic knowledge is implied in the regulation of the distribution and consumption of goods (as distinct from the specialized technical patterns of production); common-sense psychological and sociological knowledge underlies the norms involved in social relations, personal roles, and group organization. This connection may be clearly observed in proverbs, the "wisdom of nations."

So long as the cultural order has behind it the common authority of the groups composing a particular society, and particularly if this authority is supported by religious sanctions showing that it is a sacred order, the norms which it includes must be valid. Any individual deviation from them only strengthens their validity, for it is qualified as an offense against superindividual standards and its repression makes the society more conscious of the importance of those standards. And, therefore, the generalizations connected with such norms *must be true:* in common-sense knowledge "exceptions confirm the rule," for they make it more manifest to common reflection.

Take, for instance, the age-old common-sense "truth" that women are inferior to men. This "truth" cannot be doubted in any society in which subordination of women to men is a normatively regulated part of the social order, for to doubt it would mean to question the validity of all the patterns of social relations between the sexes. Exceptions merely confirm it, for any relationship in which a man—say, a henpecked husband—is subordinated to a woman is regarded as abnormal. And such a generalization can easily coexist with another emphasizing the inborn inferiority of lower classes—say, the villains as compared with the nobles. For women of the higher class are simply not compared at all with men of the lower class. There is no social need for such a comparison, since men of the lower class are socially subordinated to men of the upper class; and if occasionally a noble woman rules over villains, she does so as the representative of some man, absent, dead, or immature.

These judgments of personal "superiority" or "inferiority" are evaluative. Judgments of value constitute the nucleus of all common-sense knowledge; for there is always a judgment of value directly implied by a rule of conduct. Descriptive and explanatory judgments have mostly an auxiliary significance. For instance, historical description shows the goodness and greatness of national heroes and rulers. Economic valuations implied by the rules of prudence are supported by the description and explanation of economic facts. Psychological concepts commonly applied to human individuals are evaluative, positively or negatively, as "intelligent," "stupid," "wise," "foolish," "courageous," "cowardly," "persistent," "obstinate," "proud," "humble," "vain," "modest," and so on. Only in explaining why an individual "came to be that way" are nonevaluative statements used.

Common-sense knowledge, like technical knowledge, is thus relative to practical interests. And yet there is a fundamental difference between them. The cultural order being inviolable, it does not provoke the same kind of problem of practical control as the natural order. The individual is presumably unable to change it and is not even supposed to want to change it; the only problems he is expected to face are those of his own personal adaptation to the order such as it is. This concerns not only the average member of such a stable society but also the ruler and master of men, lay or religious. He has to adapt himself to the existing systems of binding norms like everybody else; and it is his function to maintain those systems against all disturbances, whether from individual offenders, foreign aggressors, evil spirits, or natural forces. And every individual by the time he grows up and becomes adapted knows all he ought to know about the cultural order from his own personal experience, merely by participating in it. If by any chance he needs to learn something about facts which are unconnected with his own share in collective life and about which he consequently has no firsthand knowledge founded on personal participation, all he needs to do is to ask somebody who possesses this knowledge.

The only way in which the common-sense knowledge of a society can ever become problematic is through collective opposition to the cultural order which this knowledge underlies. We say "collective opposition" because if only scattered individuals oppose it they are regarded by the society as abnormal and their opposition is viewed as criminal, sinful, or at best foolish. Nor can criticism of "our" cultural order coming from another society with a different culture raise doubts as to the validity of "our" standards; it only provokes the tendency to retaliate by criticizing whatever in that culture appears as negative when judged by "our" standards. Their language is unintelligible babble, their religion is unholy, their customs are ridiculous, their mores are wicked, their art is ugly, their wisdom is folly, and their social structure is chaos.

Opposition must develop inside a society to shake its belief in the manifest validity of its order and the self-evident truth of the common-sense knowledge that underlies it. Of course, opposition usually presupposes cultural contacts with the outside social world.[6] New cultural patterns which the opponents tend to substitute for the old are seldom entirely original creations of

[6] H. E. Barnes and H. Becker in their remarkable work *Social Thought from Lore to Science* (Boston, 1937–38), especially in the first volume, emphasize the cultural contacts between different societies which overcome their social and mental isolation, as the main factor of inner cultural conflicts and of critical reflection about the social order. This is the first consistent and inclusive historicosociological study of the genesis and evolution of social thought.

theirs: in most cases they originate in individual reproduction—with some new variations—of patterns which already exist in other societies. "Foreign" standards and norms of conduct may be imported by returning travelers, merchants, wanderers, immigrants; in literate societies they sometimes come by way of indirect communication through books and periodicals. Sometimes there has been an overlapping of groups bearing different cultures in consequence of invasion, gradual interpenetration on frontiers, or common participation in large groups drawing members from different societies, like an international church or class organization.

But in any case the acceptance of patterns from outside which conflict with the existing cultural order or (less frequently) of new patterns originally produced by members of the society do not give rise to collective opposition unless there is at least latent revolt more or less widely spread among a part of that society. It may be the revolt of youth [7]—a usual phenomenon in societies with certain types of education—or a class revolt, or a revolt of some group which is a part of the society but which does not quite fit into it functionally. However, the investigation of all these varied and complex processes would take us far beyond the scope of the present work.

When within a society have been formed two conflicting groups or parties, one of which tends to change the traditional cultural order (or any part of it) while the other tends to maintain it, thinking about the nature and foundations of this order, hitherto not only unnecessary

[7] F. Znaniecki, *Social Actions* (New York, 1936), Chap. XIII, "Revolt."

but undesirable, becomes a duty of the adherents of both parties—let us call them "novationists" and "conservatives." For knowledge can be a weapon in social struggle, although in the situation we are now discussing, when active social tendencies combating or supporting social rules precede and condition reflective thinking about the theoretic foundations of those rules, opposing parties cannot by intellectual arguments induce each other to change their tendencies. Yet such arguments have a double use.

First, they strengthen the conviction of the adherents of each party that their own tendencies are "right" and those of their opponents "wrong"; and such a conviction is a real social force. This is not so important for the supporters of the existing order, since they have on their side all the traditional standards of validity hitherto recognized in the given society and need no new arguments to convince them that they are right. The opponents of this order, on the contrary, must find some new standards of validity to believe in, for only then will their status in their own eyes be not that of mere rebels giving vent to their subjective dissatisfaction but that of fighters for an objectively valid "cause." Therefore we find critical reflection about the nature and foundations of the cultural order originating and developing primarily among novationists, while conservatives are less "intellectual" and rationalize their defense of the traditional order mainly in reaction to arguments of their opponents. This does not apply to "reactionaries," like Joseph de Maistre, who wish the return of a cultural order that has already lost its old claim to social validity.

The second advantage of knowledge as a social weapon is that it can be used to gain adherence or at least sympathetic neutrality on the part of people who are undecided or not directly interested in the struggle; and if the latter lasts long enough, knowledge may help "convert" the young. In either case, of course, appeal must be made ultimately to the active tendencies of the people whom one or the other party wishes to influence into taking its side; but knowledge may be an effective instrument in making this appeal.

However, this duty to think about the cultural order is dangerous from the point of view of both parties, for the opponents of the traditional order wish the thinking to undermine it intellectually by invalidating the "common-sense" knowledge which underlies it while the defenders wish the thinking to strengthen it intellectually by proving that knowledge to be essentially true. Now, ordinary people without special preparation cannot be trusted to perform this duty independently, for their untrained and undirected thinking may lead them astray: they are apt to commit silly "errors" of judgment which, instead of supporting their own side in the controversy, furnish arguments for the other side. Some intellectually superior and widely informed person must do the thinking for them, and their duty is then simply to imitate his thinking and assimilate its results as well as they can.

Ordinarily, it seems, such thinking for the rank and

file of novationists and conservatists is a part of the role of their social leaders. This phenomenon can still be observed in preliterate societies and peasant communities. But unless such a leader-thinker leaves a written record of his thinking, the memory of it does not survive him very long. History has preserved mainly the names of leader-thinkers who have left writings or to whom later writers have ascribed certain intellectual achievements. These range from legendary *héros civilizateurs* like Moses and Numa Pompilius, through such historical leaders as Hammurabbi, Amenophis IV, and Solon (whose written works are not quite authenticated), to men whose functions as both are certain, like Caesar and Calvin. Some leaders in modern societies still try to combine these functions—take Sun-Yat-Sen, Lenin, Trotsky, Mussolini, Hitler, and (on the other side) less famous persons like the conservative British statesmen.

Usually, however, in most complex societies, active social leaders lack the time, the will, or the ability to theorize for their followers about the cultural order. Somebody else from among the novationists or conservatives performs this function, being regarded as wiser than the others and being accepted by them as their guide in thinking about the social or—more generally—cultural problems which the actual conflict is raising. A distinct kind of social role develops which may be called by the old term "sage."

The original status of the sage lies within his party, and his original function consists in rationalizing and justifying intellectually the collective tendencies of this party. It is his duty to "prove" by "scientific" arguments that his party is right and its opponents are wrong. If a novationist, he has to prove, for example, that the traditional religious system, or the political structure, or the laws and customs, or family life, or the class hierarchy, or the organization of economic processes, or the art and literature of the past, or all of them together are partially or completely "bad" and ought to be reformed, if not abolished; and that the changes of those systems or the new systems which the novationist tends to introduce are good and ought to be accepted. Such was the function of the "Church fathers" in the first centuries of the Christian era, of the humanists from Petrarch to Erasmus (their innovations, though largely borrowed from ancient civilizations, were new with reference to the existing order), of the writers and preachers during the Protestant Reformation, of the French political scientists in the eighteenth century, of the socialist writers of the nineteenth. After a new order has been introduced, and while there is still some open or latent resistance to it on the part of the adherents of the old order, the task of the sage is to justify the innovations by "proving" the superiority of the new order over the old. In this sense, all students of culture and even some natural scientists have been compelled to perform roles of "sages" at the beginnings of the Bolshevik regime in Russia and the Nazi regime in Germany.

If the sage represents a conservative group, his duty is just the opposite. He has to show by "scientific" argument that existing cultural systems and traditionally established patterns are positively valuable, that good necessarily results from their maintenance, whereas their overthrow or reform according to the novationists' plans would have evil consequences.

To perform his function a sage is supposed to possess encyclopedic knowledge of the entire past and present culture of his own society and as much knowledge of other cultures as can be used to prove his theses by analogy or contrast. For novatory currents are seldom limited to one field of culture, but directly or indirectly spread to various fields and conservative reaction interprets collective attacks on any set of traditional rules as threatening the whole established culture.

For instance, religious struggles between Christianity and Paganism and later between Catholicism and Protestantism involved customs and mores, the structure of many social groups, including the state, economic organization, literature, and art; the economic class struggles started by the socialist movement involve all "bourgeois" culture; the political revolt of the Nazi has left no cultural standards of Western civilization untouched; even such primarily artistic and literary currents as the Renaissance or Romanticism had wide religious, social, and economic implications. On a smaller scale the same phenomenon may be easily observed in traditionalistic rural communities. The sage of either party must have all the knowledge necessary to attack or to defend by reasoning and factual evidence his party's standards of valuation and conduct in any field of culture.

In his method he must subordinate altogether prob-

TECHNOLOGISTS AND SAGES

lems of truth and error to problems of right and wrong. His thinking is directed by two fundamental postulates: that which is right must be based on truth; that which is wrong must be based on error. And "right" for the sage whose role is bound up with a group in struggle is whatever his group wants; "wrong," whatever the other group wants in opposition to his. His method consists in showing what general truths are implied in his own "right" standards and what general errors the "wrong" standards of his opponents imply and in adducing facts which validate his judgments. Of course, facts will validate them: that is certain *a priori*. All that is needed is to select the facts properly and interpret them in accordance with his premises. Because this kind of argument is not reducible to the principle of contradiction, he needs both positive empirical evidence to support his own truths and negative empirical evidence to make his opponents' errors manifest.

There is no doubt but that he can perform this task to the satisfaction of himself and his adherents, for in the vast multiplicity of diverse cultural data it is always possible to find facts which, "properly" interpreted, prove that the generalizations he accepts as true are true and that those he rejects as false are false. But his task becomes complicated by the activity of the sages on the other side, who try to prove the rightness of their standards and the wrongness of his by deducing from the former "truths" which are confirmed by facts and from the latter "errors" invalidated by facts. If his group is in power, his opponents may be simply silenced. Never in the course of history has silencing been so thorough and consistent as under the present regimes in Germany and Russia. But if there is a certain freedom of discussion, the sage must use either dialectics to prove that the reasoning of his opponents is false, or factual evidence to show that their facts are unreliable; or both.

However, sages—like technologists—sometimes go beyond their socially determined roles and fail to limit themselves to a mere justification and rationalization of the existing tendencies of their parties. They try to create "higher," more comprehensive and exhaustive standards of valuation and norms of conduct than those explicitly contained in the existing cultural order or the opposition against it. These become "ideals," with reference to which cultural reality is conceptually organized into an axiological system. If the sage is a novationist, his ideal is the supreme standard of a new order which he constructs conceptually in advance, but it is also a standard by which the actual values and tendencies of the novationists themselves are judged. The future order is to include values which find no place in the old order and to satisfy tendencies which hitherto remained unsatisfied, but these values and tendencies must be justified by the ideal. Any values and tendencies detected among the novationists which are not in accordance with the ideal ought to be eliminated. On the other hand, the ideal may demand the creation of new values and the development of new tendencies by those who will participate in the new order. To participate in St. Augustine's

"City of God," men must become true Christians. The future communist society requires new values in every field of culture and a working class morally purified of all the defects shown by the *Lumpenproletariat* as well as by the passive servants of capitalistic paternalism and imbued instead by a new type of solidarity.

On the other side, the conservative sage, who regards the existing order as satisfactory from the point of view of higher standards of valuation and conduct, does not judge it to be a perfect embodiment of those standards. He sees many imperfections, not only individual deviations from the rules but conflicts between rules and inconsistencies in the common-sense knowledge that underlies them. He discovers some group values and group tendencies which should not be there, because they disagree with the highest standards, and also the lack of other values and tendencies which should be there because those standards imply them. The traditional order is thus normatively criticized, systematized, and perfected. This does not mean that the sage desires to innovate: the essence of the existing order is right; its defects are accidents due to the imperfection of human nature. Take as examples Confucius, Xenophon, Cato, Cicero, Seneca, Dante, Fénelon, Blackstone, and Disraeli.

A few sages even try to rise above the actual struggle between conservative and novationist currents and seek supreme standards to which the valuations and active tendencies of both may be subordinated, as, for example,

Lao-tse, Socrates, Marcus Aurelius (whose role as a sage was altogether independent from his role as an emperor). But this kind of thinking (for reasons which we hope to make clear in our next chapter) is rather characteristic of scholars when they act as sages and turn to the ideal standardization of practical cultural life—like Plato, Aristotle, St. Thomas, Spinoza, Locke, Hume, Kant— than of those sages who have no backing by a school and whose role depends on partisan support.

Impartiality is probably more frequent among sages who devote themselves mainly to negative criticism rather than to positive ideological construction. In any case, it is always easier for a sage to criticize his opponents effectively than to "prove" the rightness of his own standards and the truth of his generalizations. And a critique of culture in general may be used by each party against the other; such double use was made of the Book of Ecclesiastes, of the works of the Sophists, the Cynics, Montaigne, La Rochefoucauld, Nietzsche.

When a sage, instead of merely justifying and rationalizing existing collective tendencies, undertakes the task of standardizing and organizing them conceptually with reference to an ideal, this ideal takes the place of the popular standards of "right" and "wrong," and becomes a criterion of truth and error, in the sense that whatever generalizations are implied in it must be true while those conflicting with its implications must be false; whatever facts confirm the former must be real, whereas those that seem to invalidate them must be unreal. Thus, for a sage of China the axiological and normative order

TECHNOLOGISTS AND SAGES 79

of human society agreeing with his ideal coincides with the order of the universe.[8] Only those who accept and conform to the former understand the latter; there is no conception of objective theoretic truth independent of ethical and political valuation not only as to culture but also as to nature. In the Socratic-Platonic conception, the Good is the supreme criterion and truth must agree with it; no idea can be true which conflicts with the idea of the Good, and because the empirical world is only real as a sensory manifestation of the ideal, no reality can objectively exist which does not conform with the idea of the Good: everything else is an illusion, a μὴ ὄν. For the Christian sage, "the fear of God is the beginning of wisdom" and the love of God is its culmination: God, supremely good and wise, is the source of all truth and all reality; and any theoretic judgment that presumes anything else must be either error or a lie. In the Marxian doctrine, standards of knowledge are relative to natural conditions, determined by the economic structure of society at particular stages of the dialectical historical process; the validation of Marxian theory is that it corresponds to the final stage of this process—the passage from capitalism to the ultimate synthesis of communism, and any theory that disagrees with it must be invalid.

Obviously, the role of the sage makes him unable to construct the foundations for a practical control of cultural reality. For the kind of knowledge which his social

[8] M. Granet, *La Pensée chinoise* (in the series "Evolution de l'humanité").

duty makes him cultivate is not subjected even to the pragmatic test of success or failure, like the knowledge of the technological leader, expert, or inventor. The only test which it has to undergo is its acceptance or rejection by the people who participate in cultural life. And this acceptance or rejection is directly dependent on the attitude of those people toward the standards of valuation and norms of activity to which the knowledge of the sage is subservient. If they recognize his standards and norms, they believe that his knowledge is true, because they want it to be true; if not, they believe that his knowledge is false, because they want it to be false.

Nor can the sage advance theoretical knowledge about culture independently of practical purposes, for this needs scientific objectivity, which is incompatible with his role. Therefore, with the slow but steady growth of the objective sciences of culture which scholars and investigators are building, the role of the sage is becoming increasingly difficult. For, although objective theoretic knowledge in such fields as sociology and economics can be applied to practical problems, just as objective theoretical knowledge in physics or biology is being applied, yet it furnishes no basis for the construction or defense of any ideological system: it can be used only to show how those who construct and accept this system can realize it.

And yet the social demand for sages does not decrease —rather the contrary. Not only do the ruling groups in societies with new "totalitarian" orders require all their scientists to be sages, helping to prove the validity of

TECHNOLOGISTS AND SAGES

such orders, but also among the populations of democratic countries there seems to be a growing demand for sages. In the great complexity of modern social life, with its numerous and partly overlapping groups, each having an order of its own, there are various in-group and inter-group conflicts which cannot be subsumed or regarded as parts of any universal ideological opposition.[9] The growing rapidity of change brings with it a multiplicity of these conflicts at an ever-increasing rate. The interdependence between groups and societies makes many of these conflicts practically significant for people not directly engaged in them. The spread of communication and popular education inform the large mass of the people about the innumerable new and complex issues which continually arise in every domain of culture and in every part of the world and any of which may sooner or later have some influence upon their own lives. Of course, they cannot understand those issues or interpret the meaning of the crowding events with reference to their interests, valuations, and norms. They feel the need of enlightenment from men of superior mind and wider information. And in response to this need, there have arisen thousands of diminutive sages ready to tell them from the pulpit, the platform, the newspaper column, the pages of a magazine, the radio broadcasting center, what

[9] This is well manifested in the inability of any ideological group in America to persuade the American people that the entire present situation in this country is one of fundamental opposition between capitalism and proletarian revolt, or individualism and collectivism, or democracy and totalitarianism, or nationalism and internationalism, or religion and atheism, or spiritualism and materialism, or any other such alternatives.

they ought to think about everything important that is going on in the cultural world. While such wise persons can unhesitatingly appreciate whatever they speak about in terms of religious righteousness or moral goodness, justice or artistic beauty, political efficiency or economic utility, eugenics or human welfare in general, the way they use facts and generalizations to "prove" such judgments shows that they either ignore the growing body of theoretically objective and methodologically exact knowledge about cultural phenomena or else arbitrarily pick out of this knowledge only that which seems to fit into their axiological thinking.

Often scientists who have achieved prominence as technologists in the field of nature or as theoretic scholars and investigators in mathematics, physics, or biology feel the urge to tell the human world what is good for it: as, for example, Howard Scott and Bertrand Russell. And when public opinion tends to make scientists partly responsible, along with rulers and leaders, for the common incapacity of mankind to direct cultural evolution and to eliminate the evils which plague it, there are many scientists who confess the guilt of their profession, condemn the idea of a purely theoretic science independent of practical considerations, and demand that it subordinate the "search for truth" to social ideals. We need only mention two recent well-known books written in this spirit: Bernal's *The Social Function of Science* and Lynd's *Knowledge for What?* [10] It seems

---

[10] There have been other significant attempts to show what "ought to be" the connection between science and social life; take, for example,

thus, at first glance, as if the trend toward theoretic objectivity in the domain of cultural knowledge, until recently considered one of the most marked achievements of the nineteenth century, were condemned to disappear or to weaken; sages, individually or in schools, would then rule this domain as completely as they did formerly —a retrogression that would defeat entirely the very object of those who claim that the supreme function of scientific knowledge is its service to human welfare.

8. THE BEGINNING DIFFERENTIATION OF ROLES IN THE REALM OF CULTURAL KNOWLEDGE

However, along with the persistence of the old pattern of the sage, other trends appear in modern thinking about the cultural world. In the first place, the traditional function of the sage often begins to split into two different functions, in accordance with a distinction between two tasks which was logically established long ago but seldom clearly carried out in actual life. To construct an axiological system centered around some religious, moral, political, or economic ideal is one task; whereas, when the realization of this ideal or of a part of it is taken for an *end* of planful activity, to show how this end can be attained under the given cultural conditions is another task and a very different one.

This second task is apparently similar to that of the technologist's in the natural realm; the first one has no

---

T. B. Veblen, *The Place of Science in Modern Civilization* (New York, 1931); J. G. Huxley, *Science and Social Needs* (New York, 1935).

parallel in this realm. For, since technological thinking has ceased to consider nature as a field in which "good" and "evil" mystical forces contend for domination, standards of valuation and norms of conduct do not concern the technologist as such, because they are not a part of the natural, as they are of the cultural, order. The natural technologist's function consists in seeking the "means" to an "end" that is taken for granted; the choice of ends comes under his consideration only in so far as it is affected by disponible means, that is, by the given situation. Of course, he may and sometimes does refuse to perform a task which others expect him to perform, if he judges that it disagrees with his religious convictions or the ethical norms that he recognizes as binding; or he may voluntarily undertake, with no encouragement or even against the opposition of his milieu, tasks that in his opinion will further the realization of a religious, a moral, an aesthetic, a political, or an economic ideal. But this simply implies that he makes his special role as a technologist dependent upon his role as a member of the group or as a leader or a follower in some social movement for cultural aims, not that he includes in this role the function of a religious, moral, or political sage who sets axiological standards for others to follow.

In the cultural realm, some attempts were made in the past to separate the role of a technologist studying the way to realize a purpose assumed as given without discussion from the role of the sage evaluating and hierarchizing purposes. Machiavelli's *The Prince* was perhaps the first consistent work in pure social technology: taking for granted that the end of a prince is to enlarge and maintain his power, the author gives his entire attention to the selection of the most effective means for the attainment of this end. And it is interesting to note that the criticism of his work throughout succeeding centuries has been mainly in ethical, not technological, terms. Instead of merely testing scientifically by comparative sociological methods his hypotheses that the means suggested by him would be effective for the attainment of the end he assumed, the greater number of his critics have discussed the immorality of both his end and his means.

Since Machiavelli's time, reflection of the technological type has developed considerably in various specialized lines of administrative, economic, educational, and humanitarian activities where specific ends are accepted as indispensable and planning concentrates on the means. This is now being consistently carried through in the totalitarian states: as the power of the ruling group becomes consolidated and opposition presumably is broken, justification of the ruling ideology loses in importance; all the ends of the ruling group have to be unreservedly accepted by every member of the state, and the task of scientists is to study the means for realizing them, without raising any further axiological problems.

And yet axiological problems cannot be avoided, for in cultural life any object or process which in one connection has the significance of mere "means" to an "end" in another connection is an independent value whose realization or maintenance may become an "end" in itself for other agents or even for the same agent at a different time. And, vice versa, a value whose realization or maintenance was an "end" in one connection may become in another connection a "means" to some other "end." You cannot isolate here arbitrarily one practical cultural problem and its solution from the rest of the human cultural world; you must take into consideration all the other practical cultural problems which are connected with it now and may become connected with it as an actual consequence of your activity—your own problems, those of the individuals and groups whose coöperation you must enlist, and those of the wider society whom you wish to influence through those individuals or groups. Otherwise, divergent, perhaps conflicting, standards of valuation and norms of conduct will continually interfere with the planful realization of your cultural "end." This "end" as a value and the activity pursuing it must be incorporated into an axiological and normative system organizing conceptually all the values and activities which are or will be connected with it in the active experience of all the people who are or will be involved in the realization of your plan.

In short, anyone who desires to become a technological leader in the cultural realm, rationally planning the activities of his group, needs first of all a sage to show him the place which the values he intends to use take among standardized values of their kind and what function the activity he initiates will perform among the normative patterns of his society or of mankind at large during the epoch in which he lives. The role of the sage in this sense seems destined to increase rather than to decrease in importance with the development of social planning. But, of course, this increase in importance will be possible only if sages cease to combat one another in vain and futile attempts to "prove" the validity of their own ideals and the invalidity of their opponents' and if they instead substitute in every domain of culture a coöperative, gradual creation of an ideal sufficiently comprehensive and dynamic to harmonize in a new synthesis those standards of value and norms of conduct which have already been developed in this field and which will be developing through further human endeavors. Then we shall call such sages "philosophers" in the Greek meaning of the term.

However, neither technological leaders in the domain of culture nor philosophers of culture can perform their functions unless there exists a purely theoretic nonevaluative and nonnormative knowledge of cultural reality, the kind of knowledge that sociologists, economists, religionists, philologists, and investigators of art and of science itself are building up when they study objectively *as empirical data* human values and axiological standards, human activities and the norms which regulate them, their structural connections in cultural systems, the causal and functional relationships between their changes.

The cultural leader (or the cultural expert who assists him) in his planning needs this kind of objective knowledge; and he cannot gain it by mere observation of that fragment of reality which he and his group are actually trying to modify, as the older natural technologists did prior to the development of modern sciences of nature. For there are numerous structural and causal bonds between the given fragment upon which he acts and other cultural phenomena which only a systematic science of this field of culture can discover. More than this: his own values and active tendencies and those of his group must be objectively investigated, and their structural and causal connection with the wider cultural reality discovered. He and his group are not pure rational subjects raised above the reality they are trying to change: their lives are integral parts of this very reality.

The philosopher of culture needs the results of objective scientific studies of the cultural world as material with which to build his ideal. He cannot know at first hand all the standards of valuation and norms of action embodied in the multiple and varied social, economic, technical, artistic, religious, linguistic, scientific systems that constitute the world of human culture, since no specialist in any of those fields possesses as yet such a comprehensive knowledge. Nor can he discover by his own research the processes in which the dynamic force of those multiple standards and norms is manifested, since special scientists are only beginning to investigate such processes. And yet all this knowledge is essential for him if he does not wish to spin his ideal out of the "depths of his own spirit" but hopes to synthesize in it the most significant historically and the most potentially influential strivings of mankind for a higher, richer, more perfect, and more harmonious cultural life.

TECHNOLOGISTS AND SAGES

But a fully efficient coöperation between planful technology and philosophy of culture, on the one hand, and a strictly objective science of culture, on the other hand, can never develop if the objective scientist lets his choice and definition of theoretic problems be determined by the demands of the technologist or the philosopher. Even in the realm of nature, technology has begun to follow the leadership of theoretic science and, instead of setting practical purposes in advance and then trying to gather whatever theoretic knowledge seems necessary for their realization, starts rather with the new theoretic results achieved by scientific research independently of practical aims and then seeks for possible practical applications of those results.

In the cultural realm where, as we have seen, the people who wish to solve a practical problem are an integral part of that very problem and no technological or ideological activity can be isolated from other activities of its kind, it is even more essential for the advance of practical control as well as of science itself that the theoretic investigation be unhampered by what technologists and philosophers believe they need to know for the attainment of their aims. The kind of knowledge they deem useful is conditioned by their vision of the future, and this vision is limited in turn by the kind of knowledge they have already utilized in their roles as participants in the present culture. New, hitherto undreamed-of possibilities of cultural evolution can be discovered only by objective, strictly theoretic sciences, unrestricted by any technical or ideological considerations, freely growing in accordance with their own methodological principles and systematically exploring the world of culture as the world of nature has been explored for four centuries. But this is a matter which can be better treated in our last chapter.

CHAPTER THREE

SCHOOLS AND SCHOLARS AS BEARERS OF ABSOLUTE TRUTH

1. THE SACRED SCHOOL

WHEN dealing with the origin of "scientists," we were faced by the puzzling question: How was it possible that men who indulged in cultivating knowledge, instead of being active like normal members of society, should be not only tolerated but viewed as performing a socially useful function and granted social status in their practical milieu? We found a partial answer to this question in the emergence of the roles of the technologist and the sage: scientists came to be socially acceptable because and in so far as they specialized in cultivating a kind of knowledge which men of action regarded as useful for practical purposes. It ought to be noticed, however, that unless a technologist or a sage was also a leader or a ruler of men and drew authority or prestige from his active role, his status never was particularly high among his contemporaries, however exalted his name may have become in later generations. The knowledge that is needed as a condition of success in practical activity is always less highly esteemed socially than the success to which it is subservient.

And yet, along with this purely instrumental valuation of knowledge which prevails in popular reflection, we find in all civilized societies another attitude. There seems to be a kind of knowledge which certain social groups value for its own sake irrespective of any practical applications; and these social groups must have had a considerable influence, since in many societies imparting apparently useless knowledge to the young is regarded as an important social function and institutions that give this type of unpractical instruction enjoy a higher prestige than those giving a useful education at the same age. There are many examples of scientists recognized as bearers of this unpractical knowledge but nonetheless enjoying high honor. Remember the Chinese mandarins, whose position of prestige and power was entirely based on knowledge of the classics. Among the orthodox Jews, the poor student of the Talmud has a greater prestige than the man of wealth. In France, if a member of the Academy of Sciences is invited to dinner he is given the place of honor at the right of the hostess. In Poland before the present invasion, the official rank of a full university professor was next below that of an undersecretary of state and equal to that of the governor of a province or a brigadier general.

There must be, obviously, a source of valuation of knowledge different from recognition of its practical utility; and there must be social circles which need and appreciate the scientist, the man who cultivates knowledge, not because they can use his knowledge to define

SCHOOLS AND SCHOLARS

and solve technical situations or to influence people in social conflicts but for some other reasons.

If we survey the cultural history of societies that have grown beyond the tribal stage—such as Egypt, Babylonia, Assyria, China, India, Persia, the Jews since the seventh century before Christ, the Greeks, the Etruscans, the Romans, the Gauls, the Mayas, the Aztecs, the Incas, the Arabs under Islam, European nations during the Middle Ages—nearly everywhere we find a group or several connected groups of men, usually of a priestly character (even a mandarin occasionally performed priestly functions), who transmit from old to young a more or less extensive and coherent complex of sacred lore. Because of the fundamental importance that the processes of teaching and learning possess in such groups—being sometimes, as in China, the main, if not the only, bond uniting their members—we call them "sacred schools" and their members "religious scholars." [1]

There are two possible origins of sacred schools. On the one hand, already on the tribal level, there are secret associations with several grades of initiation.[2] To be admitted to such an association, an individual must be taught by other initiates a certain amount of sacred lore inaccessible to outsiders; and as he rises to higher grades,

[1] We do not know of any general study of sacred schools. We have used for comparative purposes mainly secondhand information contained in historical works on particular religions and in synthetic studies of particular civilizations. Among the latter, we have found especially useful the great historical series "Evolution de l'humanité," edited by Henri Berr.

[2] Cf. H. Webster, *Primitive Sacred Societies* (New York, 1908).

more and more valuable "truths" are added to his stock of information. Even where learning is only a part of the initiation, which includes also various tests and trials of bodily and mental characteristics regarded as necessary for members' roles and perhaps also the acquisition of magical skills hidden from the uninitiated, it is an essential part, the more so the greater the accumulation of group traditions.

On the other hand, we find individual medicine men (shamans, wizards, magicians) teaching their successors; and in some tribal societies there are secret associations of magicians where skill and knowledge are collectively transmitted. This process does not yet differ greatly from technical training in other occupational roles. Eventually, however, in many societies there develops an essential distinction between priests as positively sacred and public persons, whose roles are institutionalized because the religious and magical functions which they perform are regarded as necessary for the welfare of society, and sorcerers or witches, who function in a private character, often performing for their clients actions which society treats as evil, and to whom usually negative sacredness (religious impurity) is ascribed.[3] Under such conditions, it becomes an essential public duty of the priests in each generation to train successors to whom their own sacred powers will be communicated and to whose care the entire religious system of which they are

---

[3] This distinction between the religious function of the priest and the magical function of the sorcerer was introduced by H. Hubert and M. Mauss, *Mélanges d'histoire des religions* (Paris, Alcan, 1909).

now the guardians will be transmitted. Thus, in every relatively large society with a number of priests, the development of sacred schools is almost a social necessity.

Previous to the invention of writing, the transmission of knowledge in sacred schools was probably inseparable from training in religious ceremonial and various magical techniques. The symbolic expression of sacred lore in writing made it significant in itself and separated the intellectual processes of teaching and learning ideas from the processes by which candidates for priesthood acquired the patterns of religious and magical activity. Everything thus symbolized becomes knowledge and doubly holy (that is positively sacred). In the first place, it is derived from divine sources, either by direct spoken or written revelation of the gods or by inspiration granted to the spiritual ancestors of the school. These may be demigods, purely mythical beings, or men who really lived and functioned as prophets or sages but have since been sublimated by legend into superhuman heroes of truth. Secondly, it is knowledge about gods and things divine or, at least, as in Confucianism or Buddhism, about a sacred order of the universe. It is not exclusively concerned with such descriptive and explanatory contents of holy writs as bear upon the nature and genesis of the gods, their relations among themselves and to men, the origins and structure of the world, the history of groups and institutions, and so on. Technological rules or norms of moral conduct as abstractly expressed in symbols are a part of the holy knowledge valuable for its inner sanctity, since they also have a divine origin and impart information about certain aspects of the sacred order of things. It is, therefore, important to learn them, even if one does not apply them. For all holy knowledge is power indeed: its very possession means participation in the sacred forces that rule the world.

Consequently, holy knowledge requires no practical tests like technological knowledge. The very attempt to test it would be blasphemous, if it implied any doubt as to its validity. This does not mean that it is not practically applicable, for it is intended to direct human lives. But, being absolutely certain, it cannot fail. If, in any particular case, it seems to fail, the failure must either be due to its misapplication by those who have tried to use it or be an illusion, a false appearance misleading those who are not aware of the real essence of the sacred order. Here lies, perhaps, an explanation of the peculiar phenomenon that in the evolution of the knowledge transmitted in sacred schools and claiming a divine origin there is a more or less marked tendency to separate the sensory from the spiritual world and to disqualify the former as illusory or only imperfectly real by contrast with the latter, which is viewed as ultimate reality. Thus, no pragmatic test founded on the testimony of the senses can have any bearing on the certainty of sacred lore; whereas only those who know fully the spiritual world, that is, only sacred scholars, can tell whether in this world an application of knowledge has been successful or not.

Nor does the holy knowledge of a sacred school depend on popular acceptance, as does the knowledge of sages.

Its certainty is indeed socially conditioned, but its social basis is the authority of the school itself as a sacred group. The school guarantees the divine origin and the faithful transmission of the truths of which it is the bearer and guardian. In earlier periods of the history of nearly all sacred schools, this authority was enhanced by mystery —a legacy of primitive secret societies. As in the latter, the most important knowledge of the school was kept strictly secret and gained by individuals in a gradual process of initiation; no adept could share any of it with the uninitiated except in the regular method of introducing approved candidates into the group. Inasmuch as the religious system of the priestly group was also the religion of a much wider group, a certain portion of its knowledge had to be shared with laymen: thence the distinction between esoteric and exoteric knowledge, the former reserved for school members only, the latter accessible to the people. But even exoteric sacred knowledge was not to be divulged unreservedly to strangers or infidels, only to those who already belonged or were to be admitted as participants into the group of which the priests were the religious leaders.

As the use of writing develops, sacred books become an unshakable testimony of tradition and an additional foundation of school authority, without eliminating at first the prestige of mystery. Holy writs remain often hidden from the uninitiated; reading and writing are not only difficult but sometimes also sacred arts, which scholars are not allowed to profane by popularization; and the true meaning of sacred books may be mysterious, to be interpreted exclusively by the elect. Even in modern times, when printing has made the sacred books of most religious groups accessible to everybody, there are still secret societies, with grades of initiation, in which the initiates of the highest order are bearers of mysterious esoteric knowledge transmitted mainly by oral interpretation of the hidden meaning of holy writs, printed or manuscript. Furthermore, the fact that a sacred school has ceased to make conscious efforts to shroud its knowledge in mystery does not deprive it yet of a mysterious halo in the eyes of nonscholars; for in the course of time, by a process of accumulation that we shall discuss presently, its knowledge may become so voluminous, abstruse, and subtle as to be incomprehensible to anybody who has not spent years in acquiring it under the guidance of masters.

2. RELIGIOUS SCHOLARS

The social role of the religious scholar is performed within the sacred school. His social circle is composed of other scholars; he has a role among them only because and in so far as they admit him as a fellow scholar. The requirements and standards which his person has to satisfy are those traditionally applied to school members; his status and his function are institutionally regulated by the school.

Of course, the school collectively depends on the support of the wider society—ethnical, territorial, or specifically religious (like an international church)—of which it is a component and which needs it for the perpetuation of its religious system. But the individual scholar in his role as school member is not supposed to be directly dependent upon or to function for the benefit of any other social circle in that wider society: nobody but the school can judge about his scientific qualifications or decide what position he is entitled to occupy, or prescribe the duties he is to perform as a scientist.

He may indeed as an individual be given some role which is not that of a scholar: he may perform religious rites as head of a religious congregation, administer a monastery as its abbot or a diocese as its bishop, practice medicine, compose and conduct sacred music or dancing in a temple, act as a technological expert or adviser in agriculture, land measurement, irrigation, architecture, and so on, interpret the customary or statutory law, judge lawsuits, be secretary to a king or educator of his children, rule a district or a province, or function as a minister of state. But unless such a role is given to him by the school and remains under its control, it is his purely individual role and the school is not responsible for it. Since, however, positive or negative valuation of the scholar's activity in external circles is bound to enhance or injure the prestige of the school, the latter tries to introduce its own standards into the patterns of those roles which its members perform outside of it and to influence their conduct into conforming with those standards.

For instance, scholarly learning in China included inculcation of ethical and political norms which the school regarded as binding for state functionaries; and a scholar who became a functionary knew that his activities would be subjected to evaluative criticism by other scholars. In other countries, whenever leaders of religious congregations, physicians, judges, and royal councilors and secretaries received their preparation in sacred schools, not by private apprenticeship, those schools standardized their roles not only intellectually but ethically, took care that none were admitted to perform them but men whom the school had tested and declared to be worthy, made candidates bind themselves by solemn oaths that they would faithfully conform with their standards,[4] and sometimes even officially expressed disapproval of individuals who later failed to fulfill their promise.

The scholar's role within the school is strictly determined by the task of the school—the perpetuation of sacred lore. While the knowledge which the technologist uses in his planning and the wisdom of the worldly sage are both personal, though communicable, belonging to the individual although they serve his social circle, the knowledge of the scholar is not his own: it is the spiritual property of the sacred school as a whole, raised above every individual and independent of him. His significance as a person consists in that, within the scholarly group, he is one of the links of the living chain by which transcendent science and divine wisdom, once made accessible to men, remain forever within their reach. He begins as a learner and is gradually admitted under the

---

[4] The solemn sacred oath still administered to doctors of philosophy is a survival of this custom.

guidance of teachers to a wider and deeper participation in holy knowledge.

If he leaves the school for an outside role after having acquired the amount of learning that, according to scholarly standards, is needed to perform such a role, his function within the school may be terminated; but his spiritual bond with the school is not broken. If he remains true to his allegiance, he becomes one of the minor links which, through the medium of the school, connect laymen of the outside world with the original, eternal source of all holy truth. He radiates the reflected light of the school in the outer darkness and thus coöperates, though in a subordinate capacity, in the school's sacred function. Furthermore, it is presumed that through him, by the prestige of his personality, youth from the outside world will be attracted to the school and become candidates from among whom a new generation of scholars can be recruited.

If the religious scholar remains in the school and shows a superior mental capacity, he assumes the function of teacher, introducing in turn other learners into sacred knowledge. The latter, especially if stabilized in writing, may in time become so vast that a scholar, even after he becomes a teacher, continues to be a learner, studying under the guidance of either living old masters on higher levels of initiation or the dead who have left their knowledge recorded in books. Thus, the social status of the scholar within the school is at every period of his life determined by the degree of his participation in sacred knowledge, as compared with that of other scholars in the hierarchical order of teachers and learners.

His social function as a scientist is conditioned primarily by the supreme task of the sacred school to preserve unchanged the original treasure of holy truths that has been entrusted to it by past generations. It is therefore the first and most essential duty of every scholar to assimilate exactly every truth that is communicated to him by his teachers and in turn to communicate it as exactly to his learners.

This duty is associated with the great importance which words and other symbols possess in sacred knowledge. In lower stages of intellectual culture, between the name and the object named there existed an unbreakable bond—real, not merely mental. The object and its name were consubstantial: whoever knew the name participated in the nature of the object and could influence it by merely pronouncing the name in a certain context or with certain gestures. This conviction, fundamental in magic, underlies explicitly or implicitly the greater part of religious ritualism: a sacred formula or a series of ritualistic gestures produces directly certain effects because between the word or gesture and the object which it symbolizes there is a mystical connection. The popular belief in the direct efficacy of blessings and curses, and particularly in the danger of merely pronouncing words that designate evil things and events, is a persistent, unreflective survival of the same conviction.

Since the knowledge of sacred schools came to be cultivated for its own sake, not for the purpose of direct magical control over reality, the early realistic view

SCHOOLS AND SCHOLARS

evolved into an assumption that between the symbols in which this knowledge is expressed and the objects of the latter there exists an objective ideational *adequacy*. Symbols are not mere expressions of human thought but necessarily and changelessly correspond to the things they designate. The extension of this assumption from speech to writing has obviously been facilitated by the fact that early writing was pictorial in most civilizations. In any case, in all sacred scholarly knowledge we find the implication that names may be true or false. Often this implication is made explicit by myths in which gods disclose to men their own true names and those of the most important objects of sacred knowledge, or men discover such names through mystical inspiration; in other cases, gods, mythical ancestors, or civilizing heroes give names to objects—as Adam did when he named the animals—and such names remain real, true names. The introduction of writing is also often ascribed to the teaching of gods, demigods, or spiritual ancestors of the school; and the written symbols thus taught are the true symbols. Besides being true, such symbols (spoken or written) are also sacred, if referring to sacred objects.

Therefore, in the processes of teaching and learning sacred truths, an exact and faithful reproduction of the symbolic expression of those truths is essential. The same truths cannot be differently expressed, for if they could be they would cease to be themselves. The use of inadequate symbols is not only error; it is also profanation both of the knowledge and of the holy object matter to which it refers. Not a sound, not a dash or a dot may be changed either by the teacher or by the learner. Thence the emphasis on memorizing sacred texts, maintained even now in Hebrew and Mohammedan schools; thence also the importance of a perfect writing skill, as exemplified in sacred Egyptian texts, in the examinations of Chinese scholars, in holy medieval manuscripts.

Because the status and function of the religious scholar are thus essentially dependent upon his participation as learner and teacher in the transmission of a knowledge that is superindividual, removed above all possible doubt and perfectly stabilized in content and expression, it is obviously impossible for him to introduce any modifications into this knowledge. Nor can he discover personally any new and valid truth that was not known from the very beginning to the first masters, gods, or heroes who revealed the sacred knowledge to their successors for perpetuation in the school. And yet it is a fact that the knowledge of the sacred school actually grows in the course of generations, as is shown by the accumulating bulk of writings, the increasing length of time which a scholar needs to become an authoritative teacher, and eventually, the specialization of religious scholars in certain branches of sacred lore which occurred in Egypt and Babylonia, in India, in Persia, in the Near East under Islam, and in Europe beginning with the twelfth century.

This growth of the knowledge of which the sacred school is the bearer seems to be mainly a response to demands made by the wider society. New problems of natural technology, reflections about the cultural order roused by social conflicts, new factual observations of curious people, strange doctrines imported from abroad, occasional bold innovations of rebels, all these penetrate into the sacred school, which is expected to deal with them. While some of these novelties may be dismissed as irrelevant or blasphemous, yet it is better for the prestige and influence of the school if it can solve efficiently and authoritatively most of the problems which bother the lay society and can subordinate most of the new profane knowledge which seems to be gaining acceptance in its wider milieu to its own supreme, holy knowledge. Thus, a second, auxiliary function is added to the role of the religious scholar: after having thoroughly learned the sacred truths which form the eternal heirloom of the school, he ought to enrich—if he can—the school's knowledge by such additions as will increase its significance for the lay outside world.

How can these two functions—conserving the tradition intact and recognizing or even introducing innovations—be reconciled? Religious scholars throughout the world have achieved it by applying always the same guiding principle: Whatever in the domain of knowledge is verily true cannot be new; whatever is new must be false. The total Truth, including all the partial truths ever to be known, was already known to the spiritual ancestor of the school—god, demigod, or divinely inspired superman. In the sacred text which he bequeathed to posterity he revealed as much of the Truth as he judged possible and proper for men to know; and the school, in transmitting this text faithfully and exactly from generation to generation, takes care that none of it will be lost or falsified. Therefore, everything men can ever know truly is already contained in the spiritual heritage of the school. But few, if any, individual men can attain full possession of this heritage. For the sacred text must be *understood,* that is, the content of every particular truth which is symbolically expressed in the text has to be adequately and fully conceived in reference to its object matter, and its inner connection with all the other truths constituting the holy knowledge must be realized.[5]

Now, as the process of learning shows, the understanding of holy knowledge comes to the individual very slowly and only with the help of the teacher's interpretations. At first, his ignorant mind is capable of seeing only a few truths whose content must be interpreted to him simply and superficially. Later on, step by step, his mind becomes enlightened, more and more truths come within the range of his understanding, his mental vision penetrates deeper into the content of each of them, and the inner bonds between them become clearer. But the possibilities of every individual's mind are limited: he has the

---

[5] The idea that all true and important knowledge is contained in sacred writs has of course been current also among nonscholarly religious believers. But there is an obvious difference between the attitude of a religious scholar who thinks that sacred knowledge included in holy writs is high above the understanding of an unprepared human individual and can be only gradually elicited by the concerted effort of generations of thinkers and that of the member of a popular sect who believes himself capable of gaining this knowledge by simply reading the sacred text.

power to reach only a certain level of enlightenment. Moreover, the mental power of individuals varies considerably. The majority can understand only a relatively small part of what has been already grasped by superior minds. By long and assiduous study, a minority can assimilate most, if not all, that their predecessors have interpreted. Only a very few can go beyond this and give a better, deeper, more comprehensive interpretation of some of the sacred truths that have not been adequately explained hitherto; but each of them can make only a partial contribution to the understanding of the total Truth as originally revealed; for the height of enlightenment of the spiritual ancestor of the school is far beyond the mental powers of any one of his successors. Fortunately, the school is a permanent group and its collective power of understanding, which increases with the successive contributions of its members through centuries, has no such limits as the powers of individual minds.

The growth of the knowledge of sacred schools is thus essentially an accumulation of *commentaries* in which superior scholars interpret for the benefit of their contemporaries and successors either the original holy texts or the writings of earlier commentators. Interpretation consists either in expounding the content of sacred truths or in eliciting their systematic connection or both. By the first method of interpretation, it can be shown that a sacred truth known from immemorial time, when more fully understood than hitherto, will be found to contain truths which lay scientists or importers of foreign ideas erroneously believe to be newly discovered or will explain facts which have only recently been observed. Thus, medieval scholars found the essential truths of Greek science included in the Bible; some modern scholars interpret the record of creation formulated in the first chapters of Genesis as including the theory of general evolution. Recent historical processes are seen to have been generally anticipated, if not specifically predicted, in ancient holy writs; and sacred ethics, if properly understood, though preached centuries ago, gives absolutely valid guidance for dealing with modern social problems.

The second method of interpretation permits the religious scholar to rediscover certain holy truths which his immediate predecessors for some reason have failed to transmit or even truths which the spiritual ancestor of the school, knowing that mankind was not yet prepared for them but foreseeing that their disclosure would come in the proper time, intentionally failed to reveal at the beginning. A scholar of superior learning and ability, or even an intellectually simple but saintly man, enlightened by divine inspiration, may find such a truth and communicate it to the school, thus helping it to complete its traditional knowledge. But there is always a possible doubt as to whether such a discovery really is a rediscovery of a truth originally belonging to the sacred body of divine lore or merely an uncertain opinion, if not an error, of the individual scholar. This doubt can be removed only by showing that there is an inner connection between the rediscovered truth and other known truths that are already recognized as dogmatically certain; and therefore that, like the latter, it is a part of the all-inclusive holy Truth which only a divine mind can know completely and which men see only in fragmentary glimpses.

Whether the religious scholar thus contributes to the knowledge of the school by showing that old truths, known to the school long ago, already contain whatever knowledge laymen wrongly believe to be new or by rediscovering truths known to the spiritual ancestor of the school but somehow hidden from the present generation, his contributions must pass through the criticism of the school, which decides whether they can be incorporated into the total body of scholarly tradition. In that, the function of the religious scholar differs deeply from the functions of the technologist and the sage on the one hand and of the religious prophet on the other hand. All of these claim and are supposed to bring something personal and original which, though not unconnected with the contributions of others, stands on its own merit: a solution of some technical problem, decisive arguments in a social conflict, a mystical message from God to man. The religious scholar's commentary is purely impersonal; and he frequently tries to prove by ingenious arguments and references that there is nothing original in what he says, for it is all based on good sacred authority. His contribution stands only by virtue of its agreement with the Truth which is absolutely valid and all-inclusive, which he can neither validate nor augment.

Of course, the historian of culture must view this entire conception as a gradually developed collective product of religious scholars who have been continually faced by the difficulty of keeping the sacred lore of the school inviolate and absolutely certain in the midst of a current of new ideas from which it could not be isolated. If we compare the supposedly original holy texts as transmitted by any sacred school (leaving aside the history of their final formulation) with the vast conceptual structure which after the lapse of centuries we find raised around these texts by generations of commentators, the real achievement of religious scholars becomes clear to us, in spite of the fact that they have persistently disclaimed it. In every historical religion, while pretending or sincerely believing that they have merely interpreted the traditional stock of sacred lore, they have actually enlarged it far beyond its narrow original limits by continually adding to it new empirical generalizations; by critical reflection, they have eliminated its naïve superficialities and overcome its most striking inconsistencies; from a rather disconnected set of myths, legends, magical rules, ethical and legal prescriptions, principles of prudence, and theoretic abstractions, they have constructed a more or less coherent body of doctrine and given it a philosophic depth undreamed of by its initiators. Religious scholars were the first to develop the ideal of knowledge as one great System including all wisdom and science, a System to which every truth ever discovered and ever discoverable by men eternally belongs. This System became to them the supreme value, the privilege to participate in it more important than all worldly power and wealth.

Since as sociologists we have no right to evaluate any of the data we are studying, let us for a short time assume a different role and as philosophers try to appreciate the significance which this achievement of sacred scholars has had for the history of human culture. No doubt, their ideal of knowledge is no longer ours, their doctrines conflict with our standards of theoretic validity; and it is a fact that they have done much to hinder the further evolution of knowledge leading away from their dogmatic views. But this evolution would have been impossible if it had not been preceded by many centuries of devoted service of religious scholars to Truth as they conceived it. They initiated one of the greatest discoveries—or perhaps one of the greatest creations—in the history of culture. Over and above all personal knowledge subservient to subjectively variable practical aims of the individual himself or of his community, they found—or founded—a domain of superindividual knowledge independent of such aims, a realm of specific values permanently subsisting in its own right, with a distinctive systematic order irreducible to any practical criteria. Such a discovery could have come at that stage of cultural evolution only by way of ascribing to "true knowledge" an inner sanctity, by associating it not with material needs or with social struggles but with a supreme, divine source and standard of all values. And this very source was purified in the process: while earlier gods were powerful but imperfect beings interfering usefully or harmfully with practical human lives, the divine entity of a sacred school—personal God or impersonal holy order of the universe—came to include all intellectual, moral, aesthetic perfection; and knowledge, regarded as a way of participating in this perfection, became a much deeper bond between this divine entity and man than the compelling magical rite or the propitiatory sacrifice.

Even if we reject all the claims of the sacred schools to the objective theoretic validity of their knowledge, the fact still remains that they have enriched culture by adding to it something that did not exist until they created it. Take all the sacred texts and commentaries and view them as you would poetry. Here is a nonmaterial product of thought, over and above the material world, which has reality of its own, inasmuch as it gives men the possibility of living a distinctive kind of life, of having experiences they never had before, of performing ideational activities never performed on lower cultural stages.

Is man's absorption in this domain of sacred knowledge a hindrance to practical adaptation to his environment, an obstacle in the way of efficient control of natural and social reality? Yes, indeed. But why must all men be "adapted"? Is there no place in a complex civilized society for a great variety of personal lives, for the inefficient speculative dreamer as well as for the sober, efficient leader in action? Why should speculation about

SCHOOLS AND SCHOLARS

God and the soul be any less worth while than the invention of a faster airplane, a new poisonous gas, or a more effective method of propaganda?

3. SECULARIZATION OF SCHOOLS AND SCHOLARS

The interpenetration of different cultures was and still is accompanied by intellectual and social contacts between representatives and members of sacred schools with different religious traditions. During the last millennium before Christ there must have been many contacts, direct and indirect, between the oldest as well as the youngest sacred schools of Egypt, of western Asia, later of Greece and Italy; beginning with the seventh century, some of those contacts are historically ascertainable until, in consequence of the Macedonian and later of the Roman expansion, they often become intimate enough to produce the well-known phenomenon of religious syncretism. Similarly, we find traces of numerous contacts during the Middle Ages between Christian, Jewish, and Mohammedan sacred schools. Furthermore, even in a society with the same general religious background, there may be several priestly "colleges," each with a somewhat different religious tradition, as in Egypt, old India, or Greece; or else schisms break up a religious group into several conflicting groups each with a priestly college claiming that its own doctrine represents the only valid interpretation of the common nucleus of sacred lore.

In such various ways, rivalry develops between sacred schools; and rivalry inevitably brings with it at least a partial secularization of scholarly knowledge. For in any conflict between representatives of schools with more or less different sacred traditions, an appeal to traditional authority is obviously not a decisive argument; and unless either miracles and magical performances or physical force be resorted to, dialectical argumentation has to be employed. Thus, there usually develops a distinction between strictly sacred truths that cannot be doubted and lay truths that may be subjected to criticism because their validity is guaranteed not by divine revelation but by human reason only.

Moreover, sometimes even the most sacred truths are not safe against the attacks of "unbelievers" but must be defended by rational arguments; and efforts to convert representatives of a different religion are usually accompanied by attempts to undermine their faith by critical reflection.

Finally, disagreements between religious schools are apt to stimulate among technologists and sages a general skepticism with regard to sacred tradition as the ultimate guarantee of truth; and sacred schools must combat this skepticism by all the means in their power, including rational persuasion, lest, spreading, it undermine their prestige and influence, if not among the masses, at least among those more cultured classes from which new generations of scholars are mainly recruited.

There are sacred schools which, by avoiding all such conflicts, isolate themselves against the intrusion of secular standards of theoretic validity. Others come to recognize these standards and try to reconcile them with those of religious revelation by showing that, if "properly" understood and "rightly" applied, they cannot conflict with the latter. Sometimes secular criteria of truth gradually, perhaps almost imperceptibly, push the criteria of holy tradition into the shade. Often a separate, purely secular school of general knowledge is independently founded, as in classical antiquity. The most frequent phenomenon, however, is the progressive secularization of special branches of scholarly knowledge. Either special schools appear, unconnected with any sacred school, or else specialized divisions of an originally all-inclusive sacred school become relatively independent and carry on their studies without regard for, though not in defiance of, religious tradition. Already in antiquity we find separate lay schools of medicine, of mathematics and astronomy, of philology, of law. In modern times such separate schools have been rapidly developing in various fields of technological knowledge: military art, engineering, agriculture, commerce, and so on. The second process is especially marked in the evolution of Western universities: originally dominated altogether by religious scholars, they became progressively secularized when medicine, law, and finally various departments of "philosophy" were liberated from religious control and functioned as so many distinct secular schools within the formal university structure, until the only remnant of sacred scholarship is the "faculty of theology," on a par with the other faculties; in some older universities even this has been abolished, whereas many new universities never had it.

While in history we thus find schools of general knowledge and schools of specialized knowledge in various stages of secularization and it may often be difficult to determine whether a particular school at a particular time is closer to the sacred or to the secular type, the distinction between the roles of sacred and secular scholars is much sharper and easier to draw. For within the same school some scholars may be devoted to sacred knowledge while others cultivate secular knowledge; and the same individual sometimes performs the role of a religious scholar in one school and that of a secular scholar in another school. Of course, in concrete cases some overlapping and mutual interference will be found, and yet the fundamental differences are clear. The secular scholar's person is not expected to be endowed with positive sacredness, has no priestly characters; even if the role is performed by an individual who happens to be also a priest, this fact is supposed to be irrelevant to his status as a scholar. His social circle is not limited or even necessarily composed of religious believers or candidates for conversion: he is not required to serve the interest of the wider social group in the perpetuation of its religious life. His status and function are also bound up with the school as a group organized for the transmission of knowledge, but the knowledge he transmits is not holy; its validity must be established and its recognition imposed by other methods than an appeal to divine authority. And not only does the role of the secular scholar differ essentially from that of the religious scholar but there are several distinct varieties within the general class of secular scholars. It will be best to consider each of these varieties separately, though of course some of them may be found combined in the life of the same individual.

4. THE DISCOVERER OF TRUTH

Every secular school of knowledge, whether it originates outside all sacred schools or branches off from a sacred school as a more or less independent outgrowth, begins with an individual discovery. A man discovers a truth or a complex of truths, hitherto unknown, which he claims to be absolute and fundamental to all knowledge in general or to a particular domain of knowledge. If he finds followers who accept his discovery and transmit it to others, he becomes the initiator of a new school. Perhaps the truths he has discovered, though regarded as absolute, will be found insufficient as a basis for the total knowledge of the school, in which case another discoverer supplements them. Aristotle is, of course, the greatest example in history of a discoverer of absolute truths who has been recognized as an initiator of schools in three different civilizations. Other familiar examples are: Pythagoras, Parmenides, Plato, Zeno the Stoic, Epicure, Occam, Descartes, Kant, and Hegel in general knowledge; Hippocrates and Galen in medicine; Ptolemy, Copernicus, and Kepler in astronomy; Galilei and Newton in physics; Lavoisier in chemistry; Buffon in zoölogy; Linnaeus in botany; Fechner and Freud in psychology.

A reservation must be made, however, when speaking

of modern scientists. Many of them had no intention of becoming scholars; on the contrary, they started as rebels against the scholarly learning of their times. But they found no ready social pattern into which they could fit except that of secular scholarship. We shall see later how slow and difficult has been the development of a new pattern of scientists' roles and how little this pattern is understood and recognized in wider social circles even now. Consequently, inasmuch as they did claim to have discovered fundamental and absolutely valid truths and did collect disciples who in turn transmitted by teaching the knowledge based on those truths, their status and function came to be regarded as essentially similar to those of earlier initiators of secular scholarship. The acceptance of a new theory for transmission in universities and other institutions of higher learning still remains the chief and final test of its social approval.

How could an individual's discovery be accepted as valid—especially in the early days of the secularization of scholarship—if it implicitly ignored or even explicitly opposed the claim of sacred schools that the knowledge of which they were the bearers, coming as it did from divine revelation or inspiration, was the only absolutely true knowledge? Neither the pragmatic usefulness of the technologist nor the socially prejudiced wisdom of the worldly sage could compare with this supreme standard of validity. That the secular discoverer's position was regarded as somewhat doubtful at first is shown by the frequent attempts of his disciples to raise his standing by proclaiming his original connection with some sacred school; thus, Thales, Pythagoras, and later Plato were said to have acquired their knowledge in the old sacred schools of the East.

Of course, the individual could claim that he had obtained his knowledge directly from the original divine source by exclusive revelation or personal inspiration. Some of the "discoverers of truth" did make such claims, among them Xenophanes, Parmenides, Socrates, Plotinus, at times even Plato. But such a claim alone would put the discoverer below the level of the sacred scholar, in the same line as the prophet whose revelation is accepted by the people not for theoretic reasons but only because of popular faith in his personal sanctity, his "mana," whereas the sacred school has risen far above such uncritical belief and will not accept anybody's alleged revelation without investigating its content and determining its significance from the point of view of its agreement with the entire body of established knowledge.

The discoverer of truth must find a new standard of theoretic validity, a standard that can successfully compete in social recognition not only with the popular prestige of the prophet but with the age-old authority of the sacred school as a social group of men who have specialized in the cultivation of absolute knowledge. It has to be a standard that makes possible the recognition of an isolated individual as a bearer of superindividual, objectively and uncontrovertibly certain truth, raised like sacred lore above technical applications and social currents. It must be a standard immanent in the truth itself and thus independent of all external, nonscientific support, accessible to everybody capable of understanding the truth.

Such a standard was evolved indeed by secular Greek scholars and has since been perfected. It is the standard of *evident rational certainty* or, briefly, of *rational evidence*. Perhaps the school of Elea was the first to apply it thoroughly and consistently and also to distinguish fully between rational evidence, as the ultimate objective criterion of absolutely certain truth, and empirical evidence which, however convincing it may seem, must be rejected if it conflicts with the former—as Zeno of Elea in his famous arguments rejects the empirical evidence which leads us to assume the reality of movement.

Rationally evident knowledge, according to scholarly epistemology, is absolutely objective, not only superindividual but supersocial. Every thinking being who has become aware of a rationally evident truth is compelled by inner necessity to recognize it as absolutely valid, even if his traditional beliefs condemn it, his social prejudices make him wish it were false, his practical interests cause it to seem irrelevant, and his senses suggest to him conflicting representations. Any opinion which disagrees with such a truth, however old and widely spread, must be erroneous, no matter what the personal prestige or the group authority of those who support it.

Mathematics, as every historian knows, furnished the first and apparently incontrovertible examples of evident rational certainty—and mathematics has since been the mainstay of the belief of secular scholars in absolute truth. But, of course, after the first naïve attempts of the Pythagoreans it became obvious that no complete knowledge about the universe or any portion of the universe could be drawn from mathematics alone. The initiators of secular scholarly knowledge had to find other rationally evident truths about reality upon which a body of knowledge could be based comparable with the rich content of sacred lore.

A discoverer of truth is supposed to be a person endowed with an exceptional intellectual insight, a rare capacity to elicit, by the sheer power of reason unaided by supernatural forces, truths hitherto unknown which hereafter will be immediately evident to any mind able to understand them. Only a person who has this insight and makes use of it for the benefit of others can become an initiator of a school. This does not mean, however, that all original thinkers have initiated schools. Some were altogether misunderstood; others gained no followers to perpetuate their discoveries; still others promulgated only a few ideas which were eventually incorporated into a scholarly doctrine but were not comprehensive enough to become a sufficient basis of a new doctrine. Nor is it certain that all the initiators of schools have been original thinkers: a conscientious student of the past finds that many "discoveries" ascribed to certain great men were anticipated or even explicitly formulated by their forgotten predecessors.[6]

---

[6] See J. Picard, *Essai sur les conditions positives de l'invention dans les sciences* (Paris, Alcan), especially Chap. II, and his summary and criticism of the views of Pierre Duhem.

To become a discoverer of truth a thinker must, first of all, be hailed as such by a group of followers who treat his discoveries as an absolute beginning of a new scholarly tradition. It is a historical role which becomes fully realized only in the course of further developments, due to subsequent generations of scholars. This does not mean that the social recognition of his discoveries is needed to validate them: their validity is supposed to be guaranteed by their inner rational evidence and therefore to be absolutely certain. What he does need for his role as a discoverer is the coöperation of his followers in drawing all the possible and necessary conclusions from his discoveries. For, unlike the truths which religious scholars find in holy writs by skillful interpretation, these conclusions are not presumed to be contained from the very beginning in the fundamental truths as originally discovered by the secular scientist: they must be derived from the fundamental truths by complex processes of ratiocination and rationally determined observation, and they therefore constitute real, objective additions to scholarly knowledge. Such development of the knowledge initiated by the discoverer requires two main types of social role: the systematizer and the contributor.

5. THE SYSTEMATIZER

No secular school can be founded without a systematizer: his is the most characteristic role in the history of scholarship. Frequently the roles of discoverer and systematizer are combined in the same personality, and the men who have combined them are the best known historically. Here again Aristotle, as founder of the Peripatetic school, is the most prominent example; but to the Mohammedan and Christian Aristotelians the old master was rather a discoverer, whereas men like Avicenna and St. Thomas performed the roles of founders of schools by a new systematization of Aristotelian doctrines in relation to the existing knowledge of their own times. Newton in the physical sciences and Hegel, Spencer, and Wundt in synthetic philosophy are other instances of the two roles of discoverer and systematizer perfectly blended. Descartes achieved only a partial systematization of his all-inclusive philosophy, leaving much for his followers to do. Similarly, Zeno, as founder of the Stoic school, seems to have only partially systematized the doctrine, since long after him a man as prolific as Chrysippus spent his life developing its various parts and aspects.

The unification of the two roles of discoverer and systematizer is an advantage to the school; for the discoverer, before achieving the task of systematization, is apt to be carried away by his enthusiasm for unknown truths and to make later discoveries which cannot always be reconciled with his earlier ones. A man who wants to found a school must know when to stop: in his function, more than in any other, *principia non sunt multiplicanda praeter necessitatem*. The fact that Plato would not stop was certainly one of the factors in the curious lack of continuity we see in the history of the Academy. From the point of view of the consistency and durability of scholarly doctrines, it is perhaps best if a famous discoverer has followers in various institutions of higher learning who develop systematically his discoveries and transmit such systematized doctrines to their disciples.

The task of the systematizer is to test the total knowledge of his epoch and civilization or—in a special school —the total existing knowledge about a certain field of reality and to organize into a system the truths that stand the test. Testing and organizing are parallel and interdependent functions. The systematizer starts with the original, evidently certain truths that have been discovered by rational insight, accepting them as absolutely *self-evident first principles* of all true knowledge in general or of all true knowledge in a particular scientific domain. Only those and all those would-be truths are valid which conform with the first principles. For any truth, conformity with the first principles means that its validity is logically implied in the self-evident rational certainty of the latter. This can be proved only by deducing the truth in question from the principles or from other truths which have been deduced from the principles.

Deduction, to be valid, has to be carried on in accordance with rules of reasoning the validity of which cannot be deduced but must be rationally self-evident. Thus, all secular scholarly knowledge presupposes absolutely valid "formal" principles of deductive logic in addition to whatever self-evident truths are accepted as the "material" or "ontological" basis of a theory. Such an ontological basis once firmly established and logical methods for testing other truths perfected, the entire true knowledge—or, for any special science, all the true knowledge within its own specific realm—can be constructed as a deductive system of rational consequences which, given the world as it is, logically follow from rationally evident first principles.

Systematization is the most important prerequisite of the scholar's teaching role, an essential condition without which he could not adequately perform his duty as master toward his disciples, as "professor" toward his "students." Those who come to study under him desire a knowledge which is more certain and more complete than the knowledge they could acquire from other sources—religious scholars, lay technologists, or sages. Once they have joined the school, their social role as learners implies the obligation of unshakable confidence in the certainty and completeness of the knowledge possessed by the school and taught by the scholar. If they have any doubts, they ought to be convinced that those doubts are the consequences of their own ignorance and will disappear after they have assimilated thoroughly the teachings of the master. The latter has a moral obligation to justify this faith of the students in his knowledge by anticipating and eliminating in advance all doubts that may assail them later in contact with other scholars or in dealing with empirical nonscholarly knowledge. The ideal of scholarly teaching requires that the learner, after having mastered under the teacher's guidance the essentials of the doctrine of the school, shall have no unsolved problems or at least no problems that he is incapable of solving with the help of the doctrine.

And the only way in which this ideal can be approached is precisely deductive systematization. By learning the first principles and the truths deduced from them in a systematic logical order, the student becomes acquainted with the most essential part of whatever absolutely certain knowledge there is concerning the universe as a whole or a definite portion or aspect of the universe and acquires absolute standards of validity which will permit him to decide forever afterwards whether any human opinion he may later meet is true or false.

This is what even now students genuinely interested in knowledge normally expect to get from their university studies, if they have been prepared for the university by the prevailing method of secondary education. The author's personal observations as learner or teacher in nine universities, the information gleaned from colleagues, and an analysis of several hundred biographies and autobiographies of people with university education lead to the conclusion that, with some otherwise explicable exceptions, a "good" student in any university "subject" wants absolutely true knowledge systematically organized with reference to "first principles" and is disappointed if he does not find it. Professors usually try not to disappoint him, being well aware that their authority as scientists within the serious students' circle depends on the apparent certainty and consistency of the doctrines they teach—unless, of course, the subject itself is unfit for scholarly systematization, as is the case, for example, with the history of literature. This tendency to maintain in schools of higher learning the old scholarly standards of theoretic validity is perhaps most clearly manifested in the composition and structure of the traditional type of university textbook, which is still the prevalent type.

6. THE CONTRIBUTOR

However self-evident the principles established by the discoverer may seem, however perfectly the systematizer may have performed his task of testing and organizing existing knowledge, the school cannot rest in the security of their achievements; for any culture within which secular schools are possible is a changing culture.[7] New generalizations are apt to be introduced at any moment by technologists, sages, disinterested thinkers and observers, or borrowers of foreign ideas. A secular school can afford to ignore such innovations even less than a sacred school, for its influence and prestige in the wider society depend exclusively on the confidence which intellectually interested outsiders have in the certainty and completeness of the knowledge of which it is a bearer. New generalizations have to be tested and, if they stand the test, incorporated into the system of the school.

A school tends to deal differently with inductive generalizations and with new "discoveries" of would-be absolute truths claiming self-evident rational certainty. The latter, especially if made by outsiders, are apt to be treated as dangerous, because they may initiate the for-

[7] The connection between social change and the secular character of knowledge has been well shown by Barnes and Becker, *Social Thought*, Vol. I, especially in dealing with ancient Greece.

mation of a rival school of thought; the task of defending the school against such a danger belongs to the role of "fighter for truth," which we shall analyze presently. The former has no claim to theoretic validity comparable to that of the first principles of the school or that of the truths already deduced from those principles by proper logical methods. Taken by itself as a conclusion from empirical data and judged by scholarly standards, an inductive generalization can be at best "probable" or—to use a less ambiguous and more expressive term—"verisimilar." The only way of proving that it is "verily true" consists in reducing it logically to some more general truths already proved valid by deduction from self-evident first principles. If such a reduction is successful, the new truth becomes a component of the deductive system from which it draws indirectly rational evidence otherwise unattainable; if unsuccessful, either the system must be adapted to the inductive conclusion or the latter must be made to accord with the system. And under scholarly standards the system has indubitable superiority over any and every inductive conclusion.

Of course, it is possible that the initiators and founders of the school—who were after all only men, not pure and perfect Minds—have either failed to discover some important self-evident truth without which the system is incomplete or have erred somewhere in their deduction and included in the doctrine of the school some generalizations which did not follow logically from its principles instead of some others which ought to have been incorporated into the system. But it would need a great agglomeration of inductive "verisimilitudes" to shake the faith of the school in the system built by scientists of recognized greatness and stabilized in the process of teaching. Whenever a new inductive generalization proves irreducible to the system, it seems much more sensible to assume that whoever formulated it erred either in observing facts or in drawing conclusions from them.

It behooves a scholar, then, to correct such a generalization: to uncover mistakes and imperfections in the observations already made, to observe more exactly the same or similar facts, to study different kinds of data for comparison, to give a more adequate interpretation of the facts, to criticize and improve the method of drawing inductive conclusions. Of course, the scholar who performs such a task from the point of view of the system and in the interest of the school usually reaches a satisfactory result and substitutes instead of the original generalization, irreducible to the system, an improved generalization also empirically "verisimilar" but capable of being rationally reduced to the established truths of the system and therefore, in the light of the standards of rational evidence, indubitably true.

Such a correction and reduction of inductive generalizations, clearly shown in Plato's dialogues and widely practiced in antiquity and the late Middle Ages, was probably the beginning of a regular function supplementing in every school that of the systematizer. This function developed fully when scholars—like that great master and model of all scholarship, Aristotle—not waiting for generalizations to be thrust upon them from the outside, initiated inductive research themselves along lines deductively indicated by the system and made their new verisimilar conclusions certainly true by the reductive method. This was and still is the function of the "contributor." It has been recognized as the first obligation toward the school on the part of every scholar who has assimilated the essential knowledge imparted to him by his teachers and as at the same time a test of his scholarly ability, enabling him to aspire to a teaching position.

Under the traditional European university system, which in the main still persists and has been largely adopted on other continents, every scholar in order to attain a scientific degree in any domain of knowledge must not only pass examinations proving that he has assimilated the system of truths which he has been taught but also make some contribution to the system. Notwithstanding the influence which in the course of the last few generations the new role of investigator in the inductive sciences has slowly but increasingly exercised upon the roles of scholars, this contribution is still implicitly (sometimes explicitly) expected to furnish a new proof, however slight, that experience is in accordance with the system recognized by the masters of whom the candidate is a disciple. It would be rank ingratitude on his part (and might result in the rejection of his thesis) if his contribution conflicted with the system. He is regarded, in any case, as still insufficiently mature to do anything really original that would be at the same time theoretically valid. Only by leaning upon the teachings of his masters can he accomplish a formally satisfactory piece of work.

At first one degree, based upon an examination and a contribution, was enough to admit a candidate to the lower rank of teacher in an institution of higher learning. Later, however, with the accumulation of knowledge in every specialty, requirements had to be raised. In most European countries, the first scientific degree entitles the candidate at best to apply his knowledge in practice or else to popularize it in preparatory schools but not to be included among the regular staff of an academic school. And every promotion to a higher rank requires a new contribution.

For instance, according to the organization of scholarly roles stabilized in Poland during the period from 1919 to 1939, there are five stages in a scholar's academic career. His first university degree, granted after four years of study, is the master's. There is no bachelor's degree; but to enter the university, he must after high school have taken a two-year lyceum course, corresponding to the freshman and sophomore years in an American college. To obtain his master's degree, he has to present a contribution made under the professor's guidance, showing that he understands how the system of general truths that he has assimilated is to be applied to facts but not necessarily so significant as to deserve publication for the use of other scholars. He is not yet worthy to be admitted among scientists, though he may become a junior assistant, helping a professor in his practical functions.

The doctor's degree requires a really new, even if small, contribution which other scholars may use in their work and which therefore must be published. A doctor is recognized as a "scientist," but no independent academic role will be entrusted to him, although he may become a senior assistant, aiding the professor in his educational functions or else teaching under the professor's supervision some auxiliary subject which students may need but in which no academic degree may be granted.

To be admitted to the body of those who maintain, develop, and transmit scientific knowledge to students, he must make a third and relatively important contribution or several minor contributions and then present himself as a candidate for the role of "private docent." His candidacy is discussed in a series of faculty meetings: at the first meeting, his biography and personal characteristics are considered; at the second, a specially elected committee presents an analysis of his scientific contributions; at the third, he has to answer for several hours questions which any member of the faculty may ask concerning his specialty; at the fourth, he must give a lecture. If all those stages are successfully passed, his case goes before the university senate and, if accepted, to the Minister of Education for approval. After he receives this approval, he has the right to lecture without remuneration for university students on any topic within the field of his "habilitation" but not yet to test the knowledge of the students by examining them and evaluating their contributions. While waiting for a chance to become a professor, he is supposed—like other docents—to publish more contributions, presumably superior to his earlier ones.

If a chair becomes vacant or a new chair is established at any university, the dean of the faculty to which this chair belongs asks all the professors of Polish universities who specialize in the given field and neighboring fields to designate the best candidates from among the available private docents. A special committee takes their answers into consideration, analyzes the contributions of all the candidates, and reports to the faculty. The decision of the faculty goes, again, for approval to the university senate and then to the Minister of Education, who eventually presents the appointment of the candidate to the President of the Republic for confirmation. Still, the new appointee remains for a time merely an "extraordinary" (or "associate") professor. Only after several years, if he has published in the meanwhile still more scientific contributions, the faculty decides that it is time to raise his status; and its decision goes by the regular channels to the highest authority of the State for official promotion to "full professorship." [8]

This whole procedure varies somewhat in other European countries; but wherever the scholarly tradition subsists—and there is no other tradition regulating the roles of scientists who function in institutions of higher learning—the whole career of a scholar depends on his activity as a scientific contributor, helping to maintain and de-

[8] We speak of Polish scholarship in the present tense, although since September, 1939, Poland's universities have been closed, her scientific apparatus has been destroyed or taken away, and most of her scientists are either dead or slowly starving. For we believe that the culture of a nation cannot be destroyed by force and that the work of scientists does not die with them.

velop recognized systems of absolute truths which the school transmits to successive generations by the process of teaching. Nor is there any fundamental difference in this respect between the structure of European and that of American universities, except that in comparison with scientific work in the latter teaching is relatively more emphasized than in the former.

The avowed purpose of this regulation of a scholar's career is to combine in every institution of higher learning continuous scientific productivity with exacting standards of formal scholarship; and there is no doubt that this purpose is achieved. No scientifically unproductive individual can become a permanent member of such an institution; while the careful criticism to which at each stage of his advance every production of his—even a popular article or a book review—is subjected by an official body of mature scholars develops an intellectual self-discipline in consequence of which his work seldom, if ever, falls below certain formal requirements.

On the other hand, historians of science—to mention only A. de Candolle and Wilhelm Ostwald [9]—have pointed out that scholarly discipline hampers originality. There is no doubt that schools in their striving for absolute certainty put formal perfection above originality and prefer a thorough piece of work which brings little that is new but satisfies established standards to an important theoretic innovation which falls short of those standards.

[9] A. de Candolle, *Histoire des sciences et des savants depuis deux siècles* (Geneva, 1885), p. 326: "Un effet regrettable de l'instruction est de diminuer l'originalité." W. Ostwald, *Grosse Männer* (Leipzig, 1905), Vol. I.

SCHOOLS AND SCHOLARS

There is a mistrust of new ideas, unless they come from men whose reputation for scholarliness is well assured; and schools have good reason for this mistrust, since in the history of knowledge original failures are incomparably more numerous than successes. But since the new role of scientist-creator (see Chapter IV) has developed, its influence is increasingly manifested in institutions of higher learning, though very few of them (and only in exceptional cases) have tried to make a place for this role in their official structure. Every such institution nowadays welcomes a moderate amount of innovation on the part of its members, provided the innovation can still be interpreted in accordance with the principle of absolute truth. It must represent an improvement on previous theories as judged from the point of view of rational certainty: a discovery of a new rationally evident truth, a more extensive and perfect systematization. The highest achievement of a scholar, after years of contributions, is to make one or two important discoveries which make the systems of his predecessors inadequate and then with the help of those discoveries to construct a better system embodying all significant and certain results of scientific work in his field.

7. THE FIGHTER FOR TRUTH

At every period in the history of secular scholarship, there has been rivalry between schools representing different systems of knowledge. The struggles between philosophic schools are best known, and justly so; for they have exercised the greatest influence upon the evolution of scientific thinking in general. But similar struggles have been carried on in every special scientific field. Even after modern methodological and epistemological reflection, accompanying the steady growth of inductive research, introduced a new conception of knowledge, under which there is no place for the old type of competition between rival doctrines, such "polemics" persist in many fields along with other components of the scholarly tradition. In biology, the fights about the theory of organic evolution raged violently until quite recently; there are still several partly competing schools in medicine; psychology is divided into a number of incompatible schools; in sociology, systems of "absolute truths" brought over from psychology, biology, anthropology, geography, and even physical science are used as foundations for largely conflicting doctrines; in history, religionistics, political science, and economics the fighting goes on as in the good old times.

The diversity of scholarly systems is difficult to explain, for its main factor must be sought in the individuality of the men who built them; but a certain gradation is noticeable in the differences between particular systems. Their "first principles" may differ radically, as, for example, between spiritualism and materialism; or while agreeing on their first principles, they may disagree as to certain conclusions deductively drawn from them; or disagreement may concern the validity of certain inductive generalizations as judged by the standards of the system. However, the intensity of struggles between schools does not seem to depend upon the degree of difference between the

SCHOOLS AND SCHOLARS

systems which they represent: disagreement upon minor points has often stirred as prolonged and violent disputes as fundamental opposition between leading conceptions. We may even venture the hypothesis that competition for prestige and influence has been a factor in making rival schools not only exaggerate the importance of whatever differences originally separated their systems but actually increase those differences by "discovering" that disagreement on some minor point implied a fundamental and hitherto unnoticed opposition of principles.

The rivalry of schools gave birth to a specific function which consists in struggling to gain a logical victory for the doctrine of one school over those of other schools. A scholar who performs such a function may be called a "fighter for truth," since to him the doctrine of his own school is presumably the only absolutely true system within the domain of reality to which it is applied. Though, strictly speaking, this function is not essential to the positive construction and development of the system, yet as a matter of fact it has had great historical significance. Most discoverers, systematizers, and contributors have assumed from time to time the role of fighters for truth to defend their own theories and to attack the theories of their opponents; some scholars even specialized in it during periods when scientific polemics were more intensive than now. The "logical" criteria of theoretic validity and of scientific systematization which we have inherited from the past and to which most of us still render homage in our good intentions, if not in our actual thinking, have been for the greater part developed and perfected, though not initiated, by fighters for truth.

The difference is clear between a fighter for truth who wants logical victory for a system which he believes absolutely true and the partisan sage who struggles for the social victory of those active tendencies which he shares with his group and which he tries to rationalize and justify by theoretic arguments. Problems of truth and error are for genuine scholars raised unconditionally above all practical conflicts, and absolute knowledge should not be lowered to serve as an instrument for partisan ends. Scholarly fights are waged not on the open forum of public opinion but in a closed arena where only those are admitted to whom truth is the highest value.

Of course, victory or defeat does have an influence upon the social standing of the school and its members, even upon their economic status. Other, nonscientific tendencies may therefore—and often do—influence the fighters for truth; but these can find expression only in ways conforming with the character of the school as a group of participants in a system of truths which they regard as unconditionally certain and essentially complete. Desires to raise one's personal status and to humiliate opponents, social loyalty to one's own group, and social prejudice against the other group may strengthen the fighter's conviction that only his school possesses a knowledge which is absolutely true and fundamentally sufficient about the world at large or about a certain part of it and may make him more eager to spread this conviction. But because other schools have similar claims, he must *convince* scholars who do not belong to his school that its claims are objectively valid, while the claims of any school with a different doctrine are invalid; and this can be done only in good faith by theoretic arguments of indisputable validity.

Indeed, the struggles of fighters for truth have contributed much to the expansion and perpetuation of the idea that systems of knowledge have a theoretic objectivity which is not only superindividual but supersocial. The scholar, to convince people belonging to different schools, cannot appeal to group authority any more than to personal interest. He must invoke the only objective criterion of validity which all secular schools voluntarily recognize and which sacred schools must recognize if they wish to compete with the former on extrareligious grounds: the criterion of rational evidence.

We say the only objective criterion. Here arises a question which seems perfectly obvious to the modern student imbued with respect for facts: How about empirical evidence? In discussing the roles of discoverers of truth and of contributors, it has been mentioned already that for scholars facts are not a sufficient criterion of truth: no empirical evidence can stand against rational evidence; and a generalization derived from empirical data becomes valid only if it can be reduced to rationally evident truth. This apparent disregard for factual tests of validity has furnished modern empiricists the main reason for rejecting all scholarly traditions. Misunderstood and exaggerated by students who ignore the history of knowledge, it has bred uncritical contempt for all "*a priori* philosophizing"; various funny stories are told and retold about old scholars speculating and arguing about problems which simple observation could have solved at once.

The scholar's low estimation of empirical evidence cannot be fully understood unless viewed in its historical perspective and on its social background. Empirical evidence was appealed to for thousands of years as a criterion of truth before secular scholarship developed. It was the foundation of the pragmatic test by which technical and later technological knowledge was evaluated; and as such it was used to validate traditional magical practices as well as innovations which really increased man's control over nature. Common-sense knowledge was seemingly based upon it; and common-sense knowledge drew different conclusions from similar facts in different communities. When contending sages appeared, each could "prove," with the help of facts properly selected and interpreted, that his own ideas were right and those of his opponent wrong. Finally, the chief arguments of religious scholars were ultimately derived from empirical evidence: divine revelation was a historical fact attested by the most trustworthy witnesses and documents, while new facts—overt miracles and inner mystical experiences—continually occurred to confirm this original testimony. In discrediting empirical evidence as such and creating the standard of rational evidence, scholars prepared the way for a scientific standardization of empirical data as objective materials for inductive theory. Without this achievement of scholarship, modern science could never have developed. Though this development was preceded, as will presently be seen, by a rebellion of empiricists against scholarly tradition, the rebellion would have been entirely unproductive had not secular scholars raised the standards of all knowledge far above the level on which they had found it twenty-two centuries earlier.

Fighting for truth has been subjected to strict and definite norms. The process of convincing others exclusively by the use of rational evidence constitutes *rational demonstration*. Every controversy between scholars begins by establishing explicitly or implicitly those rational truths which are regarded as evidently certain by both parties and presumably also by the witnesses—all the other scholars become prospective witnesses, when the controversy is waged in writing. Such truths constitute the basis of the demonstration: each party then tries to prove that from their self-evident certainty follows with logical necessity the truth of its whole system and the falsity of whatever divergent opinions its opponents may hold. Rational demonstration, viewed in its conceptual content, thus uses the same methods of deduction and reduction as scholarly systematization. But the social function of fighters for truth compels them to develop a specific *form* of demonstration especially adapted to the requirements of this function and bound up with the verbal character of all controversies.

We saw how important words and signs were for the holy knowledge of sacred schools. Secular schools have preserved the essential idea of their predecessors that words and signs, if properly used, really and objectively express knowledge; only the principles of "proper" use have been changed. Symbols have lost their mystical connection with "things in themselves" and acquired instead a new epistemological connection with objects of human thinking. They have ceased to be the means for immediate action upon reality and have become weapons of intellectual warfare, endowed with the power to compel men to accept truth and to reject error. But they possess this power only under the condition of expressing truth in such a way as to preclude all possibility of its being confused with error. In every case, men must be brought to an unavoidable choice between a *verbal proposition* which is evidently and objectively true and a proposition evidently and objectively false.

When each of the rival schools claims to be the sole possessor of all the absolutely true knowledge within a certain domain and considers the knowledge of other schools within the same domain, if different from its own, as erroneous opinion, the demonstration which aims to convince others of the validity of one's claims consists in a distinctive method of bringing one's opponents to this kind of choice. What our opponents regard as true and what our school regards as true must be formulated in propositions which are either *identical* or *contradictory*. Identity is interpreted as a recognition by our opponents that we are in possession of truth, and it furnishes a basis for further demonstration. Contradiction enables us to demonstrate at once that our knowledge is valid and the knowledge of our opponents invalid by proving either that our proposition is true or that theirs is false.

But what if our opponents express their knowledge in a way that cannot be reduced either to propositions identical with ours or to propositions contradictory to ours? Does not this imply the possibility that their knowledge is valid, even though it cannot be incorporated into our system? This difficulty is obviated by the assumption that such knowledge cannot possibly bear upon the same reality as ours. Even when our opponents designate with the same words the same data of our common experience, the real objects of the rational knowledge which they express must be different from the real objects of the rational knowledge which we express. In short, there is a "misunderstanding" between us. This can be avoided or eliminated only by defining exactly every symbol used by both sides. It is not enough to indicate the datum which the symbol designates: the objective significance of the symbol has to be strictly determined, that is, we must state clearly what ontological characteristics of the real object of our knowledge the symbol is to denote throughout the debate.

After both sides have thus defined their words or signs exactly, they may discover that their knowledge bears on entirely different objects, which means that there is no ground for polemics between them, since they represent two distinct special sciences. To avoid further misunderstandings, they will then probably agree to use different symbols. Schematically speaking, such is the logical process involved in scientific specialization. While the latter usually begins as a matter-of-fact concentration of the work of particular scholars or whole schools upon certain narrower fields within a wider and rather vaguely defined domain of knowledge, it eventually results in conceptual limitation of each such field against other fields. This limitation is usually preceded by long polemics between scholars, until disagreements come to be interpreted as misunderstandings, which are gradually cleared up by defining more or less exactly the real object matter of each specialized study as different from that of every other special branch of knowledge. Perhaps this is not the only way that scientific specialization actually proceeds; but it would be worth while to investigate thoroughly the part which the tendency to avoid or to settle by this method scholarly polemics has taken in the familiar historical process in the course of which various special sciences gradually emerged from an all-inclusive philosophic knowledge.

Of course, not all disputes between schools can be thus settled by being traced back to misunderstandings in the use of symbols. General schools which claim to possess the essential knowledge about the world as a whole and special schools whose theoretic domains largely overlap do not leave each other in undisputed possession of their separate fields. In such cases, exact definition of symbols is only a prelude to the actual debate which, to be conclusive, has to follow the self-evident formal principles of the logic of propositions. If the different theories of the opposing schools really bear upon the same objects of knowledge and the process of argumentation is logically consistent, the result of the debate must be a final, objective demonstration that one of these theories is true and the other false.

Thus, to the scientists who since the fifth century before Christ have performed the function of fighters for truth is mainly due the development of the norms of symbolic relationships which constitute verbal logic. Their work has been perfected by the efforts of those logical specialists who, realizing that words of common speech are difficult to define exactly and to use consistently, have attempted to substitute artificial signs. There have been many such attempts in the past, but they finally culminated in modern symbolic logic.

The influence of fighters for truth, however, has gone deeper still and affected the very conception of knowledge, for they implanted in schools the conviction that the structure of a system of symbols as regulated by logical principles is the same as the structure of the system of the knowledge expressed in those symbols. This led to the epistemological doctrine represented by several schools, according to which science, that is, true and systematic knowledge, *is* nothing but a system of symbols.

In following the history of scholarly knowledge, especially of general philosophy, we observe a curious unintentional divergence between the results of the intellectual tendencies of fighters for truth on the one hand and the joint tendencies of discoverers of truth, systematizers, and contributors on the other hand. The effect of the struggles between scholars has been to limit more and more the range of evident rational certainty. Not only those rational truths which each school separately regarded as self-evident first principles of its system but even those which rival schools agreed upon during certain periods came to be questioned sooner or later. In every such case, it was necessary either to demonstrate the validity of those truths, to prove them by deducing them from other, more fundamental truths which in turn became eventually questionable, or else to acknowledge that they were mere *postulates* which it was rationally permissible either to accept or to reject. In the course of time, no truths were left which intellectual insight was compelled to acknowledge because of their evident rational certainty and upon which a deductive system of knowledge about reality could be founded. By tremendous efforts of constructive criticism, the rational certainty of mathematics was salvaged, but at the cost of its ontological content through the elimination of all "truths" which might be used as first principles of a system of knowledge about objective reality. This means, in short, that mathematics is absolutely certain only because and in so far as it is an extension of logic.

There remained, indeed, the evident rational certainty of the formal principles of scientific systematization, independent of the certainty of the foundations upon which systems were constructed. But when Kant, Fichte, and their followers built upon this certainty philosophic systems in which reality was conceived as determined by the very forms of rational knowledge, and Reason or the pure Subject, as the synthetic unity of these forms, became the Absolute, another period of struggles between fighters for truth invalidated these last supreme efforts of constructive scholarship. For at the termination of this period, during the last fifty years, the logic of symbols reached an unprecedented perfection; and in the light of its criticism these systems of deductive knowledge, like all the others hitherto constructed, proved to be full of logical errors. Indeed, only owing to those errors did they succeed in passing under the cover of formal principles the various spurious truths about Reason as such upon which they founded their philosophy.

Today, from the point of view of fighters for truth, the general situation in the realm of knowledge is quite simple. Upon the ruins of the older deductive systems, one absolutely true system is rising. It is being constructed by those scholars for whom science is a system of symbols ruled by symbolic logic. While these scholars form several schools, between whom there is still some fighting about minor points, they agree on one essential point: that they are the only indisputable bearers of Absolute Truth to be found in history and that they are called to build the first and only system of evidently certain rational knowledge about the world that will ever be possible. But this is still a matter of the future. At present, while there is no true knowledge except their own, all they know truly is that, if they knew truly anything, they could deduce from it something else with absolute certainty.[10]

From the point of view of scholarship, it may be fortunate that the vast majority of scholars are unfamiliar with, and do not want to become familiar with, symbolic logic. Without being able to demonstrate it verbally—since they lack the training—they suspect that there is something wrong, not with the system of symbolic logic

[10] We might quote here a number of names, but perhaps in this connection *Nomina sunt odiosa*.

as such but with its application to knowledge as the supreme standard of truth. This suspicion appears to be confirmed by the observation of some old-fashioned scholars that, whenever specialists in symbolic logic try to approach theoretic problems other than their own, they seem to show a remarkable naïveness, as contrasted with the masters of scholarly knowledge whose theories they claim to have invalidated. Indeed, they have as yet said nothing that has not been said better many times before.

8. THE ECLECTIC AND THE HISTORIAN OF KNOWLEDGE

The intellectual atmosphere of scholarly struggles favors the appearance of eclectics, men who see something true in every school but do not wish to be identified with any because of the attacks to which it is subjected from its opponents. The role the eclectic desires to play is that of impartial judge of scholarly claims. But no school with any vitality will recognize such a role, any more than a creative school of art will acknowledge the authority of an "impartial" critic.

There is, though, another function which eclectics often perform incidentally and which gains the appreciation of all schools. They must have erudition, information about the doctrines of various schools, present and past. Of course, every scholar must know the essentials about the doctrines of other schools besides his own, inasmuch as they bear upon his subject. But as scholarly knowledge agglomerates, collecting information about it becomes a long and arduous task, the utility of which is generally acknowledged. Thus grows the role of the historian of knowledge. Originally, he is a mere gatherer of the results of other people's thinking and observation, usually interspersing his information with "impartial" evaluative judgments. Eventually, however, the task of objectively determining the historical facts, of adequately reconstructing and interpreting the theories of the past and thus saving them from oblivion or misunderstanding, and finally of tracing and explaining the historical evolution of knowledge gives rise to specific theoretic problems; the historian, from a mere chronicler of other people's search for truth, becomes a searcher for truth in his own right, with a distinctive scientific domain of his own. This is a relatively recent development, though already represented by a long list of famous names on whose works we have freely drawn, such as Grote, Zeller, Gomperz, Überweg, Windelband, de Candolle, Compayré, Lynn Thorndike, Barry, Rey, Granet, and many others.

9. THE DISSEMINATOR OF KNOWLEDGE

The transmission of knowledge by older to younger generations of scholars has always been accompanied by a certain amount of its dissemination among nonscholarly groups. Sacred scholars spread exoteric elements of religious knowledge among the lay population, either directly or through the medium of active religious leaders who had been trained in the schools. Secular scholarship not only continued this custom with respect to nonreligious knowledge but developed, expanded, and institutionalized it to an unprecedented degree. For the status of secular schools in wider society, lacking the prestige of sacred authority based on divine revelation or inspiration, could be gained and maintained either by the support of rulers and other powerful individuals who happened to be interested in scholarship or by popular support. The latter has become more and more important with the progress of political and—more generally—social democratization; moreover, once obtained, it assures the scholars a relatively greater and more lasting independence in the pursuit of their scientific work than the uncertain favor of princes and plutocrats uncontrolled by public opinion. And the way to obtain it is to disseminate widely a minimum of understanding and appreciation of scholarship.

This is a function which absorbs much time and energy; but, while important socially, it is scientifically unproductive. Therefore, scholars who are active in any of the roles previously discussed are seldom expected to perform it. In older schools it was entrusted temporarily to persons who had not yet attained higher levels of scholarship or permanently to those who had no hope of ever adding anything significant to scholarly knowledge. Thus, special roles of disseminators of knowledge developed and, as in modern times their social significance increased, the number of disseminators grew until now it exceeds many times that of scientifically productive scholars.

There are two distinct classes of disseminators of knowledge: (A) *popularizers* who spread scientific information and tend to arouse theoretic interests among the adult population actually participating in organized society; (B) *educating teachers* who impart knowledge to the young in the course of a general educational process intended to prepare them for future membership in organized society. Recently, with the development of so-called adult education, a third, intermediary type of disseminator of knowledge has begun to evolve; but the pattern is as yet too indefinite for a separate analysis of it.

(A) The popularizer of theoretic knowledge has a rather difficult task, for he must appeal to people whose main life interests are already settled and essentially practical, and who (if they feel the need for more knowledge than they possess) want useful knowledge such as technologists and sages have to offer. He cannot change their interests; for his contacts with them, whether through speech or writing, are not sufficiently close or continuous to exert a deep personal influence; nor has he any powerful social instruments at his disposal to modify the course of their lives. He may indeed try to make them see the deeper theoretic implications of whatever useful information they actually desire: this is a kind of appeal often made by modern popularizers of physical, chemical, biological, psychological, sociological, and economic theories. But even this appeal is already too remote from practical situations to make the popularizer's work appear really necessary to the man of action. If the latter needs a more thorough understanding of the problems he faces in his own occupational field, he will seek it not in popular general theories but in specialized technological sources; if he meets really important and difficult practical problems outside of his occupation, he does not try to solve them by personally applying in practice the theoretic knowledge he has learned from popularizers but asks a specialist to solve them for him.

What the popularizer really does stimulate and satisfy is *amateur* interest in knowledge.[11] This may take various forms: simple curiosity, seeking new information; a half playful interest in experimental applications of theories; an attraction toward puzzling problems; a tendency to rediscover personally the theoretic significance of familiar empirical data; a desire to make some contribution to existing knowledge; a partly intellectual, partly aesthetic satisfaction in the progressive understanding of the inner structure of complex theoretic systems; a desire to reach reflectively a general conception of the essential order of the universe as a substitute for sacred dogmas passively accepted.

Amateur knowledge obviously requires a minimum of leisure time. In the past it was almost entirely limited to wealthy classes; during the last century or so, it has been rapidly spreading. If our control of natural energy and use of laborsaving devices increase at the same rate as heretofore, the great majority of the population in every civilized country may soon enjoy plenty of leisure. How much of this leisure will be spent on amateur knowledge

---

[11] A curious sidelight on medieval amateurs is thrown by the content of popular medieval books on knowledge. See, for example, Chap. V of Langlois, *La Connaissance de la nature et du monde d'après des écrits français à l'usage des laïcs,* in the series "La Vie en France au moyen-âge" (Paris, Hachette). Compare for later periods M. Ornstein, *op. cit.*

depends partly on the ability of popularizers to develop and to utilize the various forms of amateur interest mentioned above and perhaps even more on the continued efforts of all disseminators of knowledge to raise the popular prestige of a practically disinterested pursuit of science, as compared with other activities that may be performed in leisure time.

The works of popularizers, to be successful, must deviate considerably from the difficult standards of genuine scholarship. This is generally recognized; and scholars, especially younger scholars in institutions of higher learning, are not encouraged to do much popularizing, lest it impair their intellectual discipline. On the other hand, popularizers have had a certain influence upon scientific literature. Many scholars try to reconcile a high level of thinking with clearness and simplicity in the expression of the results of their thinking. This has been most effectively achieved in traditional French scholarship, where all the difficulties and intricacies of theoretic work are kept from the public gaze, as the *cuisine scientifique* in which only specialists are supposed to be interested, while ordinary listeners or readers are presented with a perfectly finished and easily digestible product.

(B) Much more important than popularizers, especially in the modern history of culture, have been teachers in educational institutions for children and adolescents where pupils are prepared not for a scholarly career but for general participation in social life, though a few of them may later specialize in knowledge and become scholars. To understand fully the role of such a teacher, a clear distinction must be drawn between the learned school with which we have hitherto been dealing and the generally educative school. In antiquity, the former was typically represented by schools of philosophy in the classical period and the Museum of Alexandria in the Hellenistic period; the latter by those educational centers where boys received training in gymnastics, military drill, music and poetry, reading, writing, and counting. In modern times, continental European universities and American graduate schools clearly belong to the first class, primary and secondary schools both in Europe and in America, to the second class; while American colleges represent an intermediary type. It is curious that the word "school" in its popular use has almost lost its first significance. In British and American encyclopedias under this word little, if any, mention will be found of scholars and scholarships.

Of course, the learned or "academic" school also performs an educational function, in that learners are being prepared for certain social roles. But the preparation it aims to give is entirely intellectual and destined exclusively for those who in their occupational roles will particularly need a mental equipment high above the level regarded as normally desirable for all socially active people. A secular university is an association of mature persons in which professors have positions of authority. Although, like every social group, it exercises some control over the conduct of its members, yet it does not try to educate them physically or morally, to guide their personal evolution so as to make them fit for social participation, since it presumes that this has already been done during their childhood and early youth. What binds this group of professors and students together is knowledge as such—the scholarly type of theoretic, systematically ordered, absolutely true knowledge. Its cultivation and perpetuation is the primary task of the group and the chief reason of its existence: if it ceased to perform this task, it would also cease to be a center of higher intellectual education. No matter what psychological motives induce particular individuals to seek admission to the group, so long as they are its members they are bound to accept its appreciation of knowledge as the highest common value.

In other words, the school of higher learning performs the specifically social function of an educational institution only because its main activities are not social but scientific, do not aim to contribute to the maintenance of the social order but to the maintenance of knowledge as a supersocial domain of culture supremely valuable in itself. Therefore, the chief personal duty of every member is to share in the activities by which knowledge is maintained, even if only by faithfully assimilating that relatively small portion of knowledge which is transmitted to him during the period when he is a mere student.

The school of general education, on the contrary, as an institution of the modern society serves directly the maintenance of social order—whether it be a traditional static order or a more or less dynamic new order. It does this by preparing the young and socially immature to assume on reaching maturity the roles of members of the society which it serves and to coöperate with the present mature members. The educational preparation given in the school supplements that which each pupil receives in the family, since the primary educational function is a part of the social relation between parent and child. The total educational process to which an individual is subjected is subdivided into particular processes in the course of which the educand acquires various specific skills and capacities which society requires of its mature members and which specialists in education are supposed to impart more efficiently than parents.

Among these skills and capacities imparted to the pupils of an educative school are some theoretic disciplines. The young, as they advance in mental development, are taught the elements of certain branches of scholarly knowledge. The content of this knowledge is predigested by the teachers, and its systematic form is adapted to the psychological possibilities of youthful understanding; but it is still theoretic knowledge, presumed to be absolutely true and valuable apart from any practical applications.

The educative school does not cultivate this knowledge for its own sake but teaches it only for the sake of the pupils, who are expected to gain from it a certain amount of information and a certain degree of intellectual capacity regarded as desirable in their future roles as members of the wider society. In the organization of the school as a group and in the consciousness of its social milieu little distinction is made between the role of the teacher of a scholarly "subject" and that of an instructor who trains the pupils in technically useful or sportive skill or that of a moral educator who supervises their conduct: they all presumably act for the personal progress of the young and thus for the future welfare of society. And yet there is an essential difference, for the teacher of pure knowledge is the only link which connects this type of school with the learned school.

The teacher was at some time associated, even if only in the role of learner, with the body of scholars who ceaselessly search for absolutely true knowledge and relentlessly demand that every particle of it, once found, be forever preserved for the future use of men. And his association with this body did not end, like that of most students who after a period of learning leave the academic school for practical pursuits, with the assimilation of the knowledge that was given to him. For the privilege of having been admitted to share in the treasure which they guard he amply repays the scholars by continuing to serve throughout his life not only society but also truth. By implanting in young minds seeds of the true knowledge as understood in scholarly circles and making them see its absolute validity, he spreads far beyond the precincts of learned schools respect for truth and regard for its bearers. He is one of those to whom pure disinterested knowledge mainly owes whatever support it gets in democratic societies.

Let us now indulge again for a brief moment in philosophic evaluation instead of sociological research. Leave aside superficial prejudices, pragmatic or positivistic, against the secular scholarship of the past, and do not be misled into thinking that, because modern scholarship has incorporated the great results of the last three or four centuries of scientific investigation, the inner structure of the knowledge that is perpetuated in academic schools is essentially different from what it was before Newton. The concept of absolute truth; the deductive systematization of scientific discoveries and contributions; the principle of contradiction as a guide in choosing between different theories: they still explicitly or implicitly dominate the kind of knowledge which the majority of professors have been taught to cultivate and in turn transmit to their students, which all faithful, hard-working students wish to be taught, and which disseminators spread among adult amateurs as well as among youthful beginners, adapting it to their nonscholarly understanding. A methodologist imbued with the new spirit of modern creative exploration and looking toward the future evolution of science rather than toward its finished results will certainly refuse to be bound by those standards and principles of classical scholarship. But a philosopher of culture cannot fail to acknowledge the enormous debt which mankind owes to secular scholars.

They have made theoretic knowledge a completely autonomous domain of objective intellectual culture. Though to sacred scholars knowledge was already a supremely valuable realm of spiritual reality, yet its independence of subjective practical tendencies, personal and collective, had been gained only by incorporating it into the religious domain and subordinating it to mystical dogmas. Secular scholars have struggled for ages to make it fully independent, ruled only by its own intrinsic standards of validity. In this struggle their opponents did not always limit themselves to spiritual weapons; and it has remained justly famous in history not only because of its victorious results but also because of the personal heroism of many of the fighters for intellectual freedom. But they could never have fought with such persistence and self-sacrifice nor won such brilliant victories if they had not believed that they—not the religious scholars—were in possession of absolute truth, that any doctrine which claimed to be knowledge, whatever its alleged origin, should be judged on its intrinsic merit by the standards of its own rational evidence and logical consistency and if not demonstrably true condemned as false.

This does not mean that their work has a merely historical significance and that, having played its part in the evolution of knowledge, it belongs irrevocably to the past. The theoretic systems they have built are still there, accessible to everybody, a great wealth of cultural products agglomerated through twenty-five centuries. We often find nowadays among scientists and even historians of knowledge the assumption that in order to do justice to achievements of past scholarship, it is enough to pick out of the total wealth such elements as can be still adjudged valid in the light of present science—observations which have been confirmed by later discoveries and generalizations which partly anticipated some modern theories; the remainder is just a mass of curious historical data. This is a very old procedure, characteristic of the scholar-eclectic but long scorned by other scholars. A scholarly system cannot be broken up into fragments without losing its very identity, and none of its fragments has theoretic significance apart from the whole. "Knowledge is real only as a system," said Hegel, whose own system is an epitome of scholarship. Anybody who wishes to understand a product of scholarly thought must reproduce it in its total composition and structure by following the thought of its makers. The distinction between the eclectic and the reconstructive approach to past knowledge is well illustrated by the works of two famous historians: Abel Rey, to whom only those past thoughts and achievements are worth considering which anticipate and promote physicomathematical science; and Maurice Granet.

Is the effort of reproducing worth while? There are two sides to this question: an objectively scientific and a personal side. We may wonder whether the systems of the past whose place in human thinking has been taken by new theories have any objective scientific bearing left or are altogether irrelevant to further scientific progress. We shall try to show in the next chapter how the new conception of knowledge which is being developed by modern scientist-investigators solves this alternative. Irrespective, however, of its solution, it may be asked whether the study of past systems of knowledge can be of help to the present scientist in his own intellectual development. We unhesitatingly and emphatically answer in the affirmative. A specialist whose intellectual horizon is limited to the problems which are actual at the time in his narrow field may under the inspiration of creative leaders do some valuable work that will be utilized by others and thus contribute to the advance of science. But no individual can be a genuinely creative scientist who is not a thinker trained by following great models of systematic and critical thought and who is not aware that his own work, however important, is but a very small part of the vast, strenuous, infinitely varied and steadily growing production of numberless workers, past, present, and future.

The question of the significance of scholarly knowledge for personal intellectual development brings us to what is perhaps the most important historical function of learned schools and scholars. They have initiated and spread in civilized societies the deeply stimulating conviction that man, the individual man, this ephemeral being dependent on his natural milieu for his bodily life and on his social milieu for his spiritual life, can alone and unaided by any divine grace or revelation reach in thought the Absolute, discover the ultimate nature of the world and his own nature. Illusion be it—but a noble illusion! And by no means illusory are its consequences. For if such is the essence of true knowledge, then the possession of true knowledge or even disinterested striving for pure truth gives man a transcendent worth, an inner superiority far above the ignorant and the despiser of knowledge, however powerful and practically influential, however wealthy in worldly goods. No wonder that the genuine scholar is proverbially negligent and forgetful in everyday practical matters, lives in seclusion from political struggles, is satisfied with a very modest economic status.

But this does not mean that secular scholarly knowledge makes men unfit for practical life. On the contrary, the man who has successfully striven for pure truth without regard to its practical use and whose knowledge is systematically organized by strictly theoretic standards, if he turns his thought to practical problems, will be better able to solve them than a man who has learned only what he needed for his practical purposes.

These are the ideas which have increasingly permeated our entire school organization on all levels, in spite of competition from other beliefs. The conviction that secular theoretic knowledge is the most important part of personal culture and that personal culture raises man's inner worth and makes him more valuable to society is manifested in the fact that the process of democratization has been everywhere—in America more than anywhere else—accompanied by the spread of an ever higher and broader intellectual education, admitting the masses to a growing share in disinterested general knowledge. And the scholarly claim that the acquisition of systematic theoretic knowledge is a better preparation for practical leadership than the kind of education in which knowledge is treated as a mere instrument for practice has led to a progressive academization of the preparatory training for professional roles. In law, medicine, surgery, military and civil engineering, architecture, agriculture, forestry, animal husbandry, finance, commerce, diplomacy, social work, and so on, important and responsible functions are mainly, if not exclusively, entrusted to people who during childhood and early youth were taught for the most part theoretic subjects with little or no bearing on their future occupations and later had several years of academic instruction in which practical knowledge is treated as an application of a fundamental body of systematic scholarly knowledge.

This could never have happened if training for occupational roles had remained in the hands of practical people, since practical people for the last seven or eight centuries have been continuously complaining about all that useless knowledge which candidates for professional roles had to acquire in academic schools before they were allowed to participate in active life. No doubt, practical people are right in a way; for the systematic organization of knowledge as taught in learned schools is radically different from that which a man must acquire to be occupationally efficient. But if practical people had had their way, professional instruction would have remained in the stage of medieval apprenticeship. If it has not, it is because all teaching has been in a steadily growing measure directed by secular scholars who are convinced that knowledge, though not itself power, gives power because and only because it is pure theory, an objective system of truths, and man must know reality truly in order to control it effectively.

CHAPTER FOUR

THE EXPLORER AS CREATOR OF NEW KNOWLEDGE

1. THE EMERGENCE OF A NEW PATTERN

ALL NEW developments in the history of knowledge have been due to those scientists who did more in their social roles than their circles wanted and expected them to do.

Among the technologists some leaders took risks and compelled or enticed their followers to participate in difficult collective tasks where success was uncertain; some experts raised and solved practical problems in which the leaders who employed them were not interested; free inventors thrust upon an unwilling social environment disturbing new patterns of technical action. By such spontaneous individual exertions, technological knowledge has advanced from the Late Stone Age level to its present height.

Among the sages were a few who, instead of merely justifying the actual tendencies of their groups and combating those of their opponents, set up cultural ideals as standards of valuation and guides of action, and thus initiated human efforts to direct cultural evolution by reflective thought.

Some of the scholars, instead of merely receiving and

transmitting the traditional doctrines of their schools, developed, reorganized, expanded these doctrines or founded new schools; and in so doing made knowledge systematic and objective, with a validity independent of any extraneous demands and founded entirely on its own rational, theoretic order.

Probably in every other field of culture development occurs similarly by the agency of individuals who in their specific roles do more than is socially expected of them. Often, but not necessarily, this involves them in a conflict with their social environment: not all innovators are rebels, nor are all rebels innovators, by far.

Now we come to an extremely interesting phenomenon for which there is no precedent and no parallel, except perhaps in modern poetry and art. We find individual scientists who specialize, so to speak, in doing the unexpected. They may be metaphorically termed *explorers,* for they are seeking in the domain of knowledge new ways leading into the unknown. Originally they were for the most part aberrants from socially recognized ways. Some of them, however, have attempted to have this type of activity recognized as a regular social function and to construct a new pattern of the scientist's social role, implying a new conception of knowledge itself. So long as they remained isolated from one another, they were unsuccessful; but with the growing facilities of communication, their number slowly increased. The first initiators found followers in various intellectual centers and eventually there developed a world-wide solidarity of explorers in every scientific field.

Thus, an individual who performs this kind of activity at the present time finds understanding and recognition of his role, at least among his colleagues. In the circles of technologists and scholars, his function is usually recognized *ex post,* by a belated validation of those results of his exploration which have been found practically applicable or have remained unchallenged long enough to be considered reasonably certain and thus fit to be taught to students. In the wider society, popularizers of knowledge manage to stir interest in some of his results by surrounding them with the halo of sensational novelty, though such interest passes as quickly as all fads and most fashions.

However, only a few institutions especially organized for scientific research acknowledge his social role as different from other scientists' and grant him an independent status. Usually, unless possessed of hereditary wealth or endowed by a rich amateur, he is forced to perform the role of technologist or scholar, indulging in scientific exploration during his leisure time. Such material equipment and economic resources as are necessary in his field are given him primarily for technically useful or teaching purposes, and only after these have been attained can the surplus, if any, be used for free personal research. But even this is great progress as compared with the time not far distant when explorers were distinctly not wanted either in technological or in scholarly circles.

Still more vague than the conception of the explorer's function and status is the idea of the personal qualifications required for this new role of his. In scholarly tradition the study of scientific thinking has been limited to the intellectual activities which are manifested in deductive systematization and verbal disputation; and even these have been investigated only with reference to their conformity or conflict with the rules of deductive logic, gradually identified with symbolic logic. In modern times, inductive thinking has attracted considerable attention, but even here most studies have centered upon the logical validation of inductive studies. Logicians have drawn a sharp dividing line between the logic of science, clearly circumscribed and well ordered, and an indefinite, chaotic discipline called the psychology of knowledge, which—according to them—has nothing to do with questions of validity. Since modern logic, if concerned with thinking at all, deals only with that kind of thinking which establishes valid relationships between concepts expressed in exactly defined symbols, all other kinds of intellectual activity of human individuals, including the formation of concepts, are left to psychologists or to those philosophers who—like J. S. Mill, Ernest Naville, Wundt, Dewey, Le Roy—do not recognize this dividing line, however much their theories may otherwise differ from one another.

But psychologists and philosophers have not yet distinguished clearly between the different types of scientific thinking which are required of scientists in different social roles and methodically developed in the course of their preparation for those roles. For instance, Wundt's theory (as exposed in the three volumes of his *Logik*) is based upon the thinking of scholars, especially of systematizers and contributors; Dewey studies the kind of thinking typical of technologists, treating it as representative of all scientific thinking. Especially vague are still most studies dealing with the intellectual activity of theoretic exploration, although every important step in the progress of modern science is ascribed to it and it has therefore attracted considerable attention.[1]

The reason for this vagueness is not far to seek. Intellectual activity must be studied with reference to the objective structure of the science of which it forms a part. Explorative thinking—though scattered rudiments of it may be seen among older scholars, technologists, even sages—is actually a new type of scientific thinking, which has probably not yet reached its full development. Its essential and distinctive characteristic, as compared with other types, cannot be discovered unless it is taken in connection with the objective structure of the new kind of knowledge which the explorers are creating. And even among them, only a few are yet fully aware of all the revolutionary implications of their collective work. The very standardization of this new type of thinking is far from completed. There is no "logic" of creative thought; there

[1] J. Picard, in the book mentioned above, gives perhaps the most complete analysis of the psychological processes involved in creative scientific thinking, though he does not take into account the contributions of James and Dewey. As to the social factors of scientific innovation, he quotes A. Rey: "Il n'y a rien que de très vague sur la question des facteurs sociaux de l'invention. . . . Tout travail positif sur ce point est encore à faire" (p. 54). This author, who applies to science the formula by which H. Taine tried to explain art (race, milieu, moment) has not contributed much to the latter problem.

are no principles of the search for new knowledge comparable to the principles of the systematization of ready knowledge. Books on methodology contain mainly technical rules of handling data, like those of comparative observation, experimentation, or mathematical calculation. And we lack completely any educational method for preparing future explorers for their function: we are unable to answer the question of why and how some of the individuals who have been taught in learned schools or trained under the guidance of technologists become original and independent theoretic explorers.

2. THE DISCOVERER OF FACTS

The first stage in the development of scientific exploration is the search for new and unexpected facts, that is, for empirical data hitherto unknown to scientists and not anticipated in their theories. Many explorers do not go beyond this stage; they regard the discovery of new facts as the most important scientific achievement.

The term "fact-finder" could be used to designate them, if it had not a somewhat contemptuous connotation. The expression "discoverer of facts" is nonevaluative and has besides the advantage of denoting both an analogy and a contrast between this kind of scientific activity and the scholarly function of the "discoverer of truth."

In the history of every inductive science there have been periods of extensive search for unknown data, which were also periods of intellectual revolt against the stabilized technology of recognized leaders and experts, the self-assured wisdom of official sages, and doctrines taught by scholars as absolutely true.

Every one of these scientists desires "new" facts, facts he has not already observed, provided they are such as he expects them to be. Their essential character must be known to him in advance, for he wishes all the facts he has to deal with in the performance of his function to prove helpful for the achievement of his task; or, at least, he wants to be sure that none will interfere with this achievement.

The technological leader desires factual knowledge which he can utilize in making his plans and controlling their realization. If his plans were entirely undetermined, he might welcome any kind of new facts. But they are not: his social role gives a definite direction to his leadership and limits the range of his planning. His plans must follow certain patterns compatible with the social conditions under which he acts. The discovery of unforeseen facts within the range of his activity may show that the latter is not so rational as he and his followers believed it to be, that the means he chooses are wasteful, that his successes must be ascribed to favorable circumstances rather than to careful planning, or that the realization of his plans is followed by some undesirable and hitherto unsuspected aftereffects. Any such discovery is apt to undermine his status or be used by his rivals and competitors for planning more efficient than his own. As to technological experts, since their type of specialized research is determined by what men in power wish to know, it may be quite dangerous for their role to indulge in seeking for new data without knowing more or less what they will find: they may discover facts which from the point of view of men in power had better have remained unknown. Many an expert has been made to suffer for such unwelcome discoveries.

The sage, as we have seen, wants only facts that he expects to use in his arguments for his side in social conflicts or against the opposite side. Unexpected facts may, contrarywise, furnish material which his opponents will use in the arguments against his side. It is not so bad if the opponents themselves find such facts, for they are known to be partial, and their factual evidence can be invalidated on that ground. But facts discovered by impartial observers cannot be so easily swept away. Therefore, impartial seekers for unknown facts in the social field are viewed as unsafe people by both sides in a social conflict; and if either side be victorious, it bars free impartial observation almost as carefully as ideological opposition.

Scholars—especially secular scholars—are not averse to new and unexpected facts, so long as the system of the school is in the formative stage of discovery of new truths and fundamental systematization: new facts are even welcome to illustrate and exemplify new truths or to help disclose the errors of older schools; nor is there any danger that empirical evidence might prove an obstacle in building the system, for it will be interpreted in the light of rational evidence. We know, for instance, about the assiduous search for unknown biological facts which Aristotle carried on for years with the help of a large staff of assistants, who collected data in various countries. Albert the Great, the teacher of St. Thomas, was famous for his factual explorations; so was Descartes. The scientists of the nineteenth century who, even if they began as explorers, developed into founders of schools were eager for new facts, while they were building their systems: take the enormous mass of materials used by Wundt in psychology or by Herbert Spencer in sociology.

However, as the system becomes stabilized and extended by successive additions, the search for new and unexpected facts not only abates but becomes more and more unwelcome. Contributors, as we have seen, must take care that generalizations based on facts within the domain of the school's knowledge be reducible to the system. Inductive "verisimilitudes," if thus reduced, become accepted as certain truths, necessary and universal. Thus, the stabilization and progressive extension of the system means that the school is committing itself to uphold as absolutely true a growing number of generalizations about empirical facts. An unexpected new fact may disagree with such a generalization and thus invalidate it, since no exceptions are possible to a necessary and universal truth. It may be saved at the cost of necessity and universality: the judgment "Some S are P" may be substituted for "All S are P." But this means that the attempt to reduce it to the rationally evident truths of the deductive system was an error; and it breaks the chain of deductive reasoning, makes a further extension of the system in this direction impossible, whereas if the school assumes that the exception is only apparent and can be explained by some universal truth yet unknown, it risks the danger that this unknown truth, once discovered, will conflict with the system. Schools generally welcome factual exploration only if it upsets the theories of other schools.

It is thus obvious that a discoverer of facts, freely roaming in search of the unexpected, has no place in a milieu of scientists with well-regulated traditional roles. He may be a solitary, independent individual with no interest in professional traditions or else a rebel against established intellectual authority. Neither of these types is actuated merely by curiosity or by the desire for adventure. Curiosity alone does not make men search for facts objectively unknown, not yet observed by other investigators: on the contrary, it is rather stimulated by social communication in which the individual learns from other people about data unknown to him but known to them. As to the "spirit of adventure," it may indeed lead the individual into unexplored fields but in search not of objective facts to be recorded for scientific use but only of extraordinary personal experiences. Tourists, wild-game hunters, prospectors, pioneers, and colonists are not scientific explorers.

Other tendencies must be active in factual exploration. The solitary observer of nature, like Fabre or Thoreau, or of culture, like those archeologists and ethnologists who initiated intensive studies of various past or exotic civilizations, is animated by love for the factual domain which he investigates. He experiences aesthetic joy in contemplating every particular new phenomenon which his search discloses; and this joy alternates with a deeply thrilling consciousness of the inexhaustible wealth of his domain, the innumerable mysteries it conceals, and the possibilities of new discoveries which it provides. This kind of love can rise to a mystical enthusiasm, as with Giordano Bruno, who, though treated as a rebel, remained primarily a passionate lover of the infinite empirical world which to him offered marvels enough to contemplate through eternity.

Some of this aesthetic and intellectual thrill will probably be found in the lives of all discoverers of facts, though in the rebellious type social tendencies seem to predominate. The latter is mainly desirous to throw off the intellectual yoke of professional science. Often he is an unsuccessful technologist, sage, or scholar who could not or would not conform with traditional requirements, sometimes a rank outsider, a self-taught amateur. His rebellion, however, is not a mere personal problem of subjective misadaptation. It becomes depersonalized and objectified as a problem of the validity of the very knowledge cultivated in those scientific circles against which he revolts. He tries to undermine this validity by discovering facts hitherto unknown which will conflict with recognized generalizations.

This is how, for example, in preclassical Greece and again in the fifteenth century revolt against traditional theories of the universe, supported at the time by sacred schools, partly manifested itself in geographical exploration; and how later ethnographical exploration often accompanied the rebellion against the complacent ethnocentrism of religious, ethical, political thought. Historical exploration frequently had its first source in revolt against myths and legends which sublimated the origins of the existing social order; later historical doctrines, as taught in school and presenting a schematized and idealized reconstruction of the past, gave rebels a chance to undermine scholarly authority by uncovering historical facts which radically conflicted with this reconstruction. Even now "debunking" is sometimes the chief aim of historical fact-finders.

The wide interest in new or forgotten astronomical, physical, chemical, and biological facts which during the fifteenth, sixteenth, and seventeenth centuries spread over Europe was largely a manifestation of intellectual revolt against all scholastic knowledge, irrespective of the differences between schools. Learned schools were aware of this and opposed the current of factual exploration as long as they could.

Since the middle of the nineteenth century, discoverers of facts have been many and active in psychology, sociology, economics, and political theory. Psychology had always been a scholarly discipline, a part of general philosophy, and, though recently specialized, had preserved the tendency to scholarly stabilization of new theories. Sociology and economics had barely emerged from a stage when thinking in these fields was done mainly by sages. They were still struggling for recognition as branches of objective academic knowledge and sought to gain this recognition by building scholarly systems founded on rationally evident principles. Political theory, though since Plato an acknowledged and important part of scholarly tradition, was shown during the struggle for democracy and later for socialism to be dependent on political ideologies and far removed from theoretic objectivity. Every attempt at systematization in these fields was followed by an opposition which expressed itself, first of all, in a search for unknown and unexpected facts which could invalidate the system.

The rebellious discoverer of facts is not a system-builder himself; he does not tend to substitute new theories for those he upsets. He finds, therefore, easy recognition among other searchers for unknown facts, since to him and to his fellows facts are objective empirical data, which as such do not conflict with one another. Subjective experiences of an objective datum may disagree; but discoverers of facts are not naïve empiricists of prescholarly days. Only data about which all competent observers agree constitute scientific facts that can be successfully used as objective empirical evidence against the standard of rational evidence to which scholars appealed in depreciating primitive empiricism. Discoverers of facts have been therefore greatly interested in standards of scientific observation. Indeed, the formation of such standards, including the invention of instruments with the help of which human powers of sensory observation have been multiplied and "subjective" variations of individual experiences excluded or measured, constitutes the main historical achievement of discoverers of facts.

A fact—as they view it—when properly observed remains a fact forever. New discoveries can supplement it by additional facts, results of even more precise and detailed observations, but they cannot invalidate it. Facts are all that is certain in any domain of knowledge. Opposition against old theories and unwillingness or incapacity to build new theories crystallize among the discoverers of facts into a norm which condemns all "theorizing."

But facts accumulate indefinitely at an ever-increasing rate, as searchers for hitherto unknown empirical data penetrate into every field of science. These facts must somehow be ordered; otherwise man would be lost amongst their enormous mass and variety. From the point of view of radical objective empiricism, their ordering assumes a significance similar to that of the description and classification of collections in a museum: it serves to guide the observer. Such is, indeed, the conception of knowledge developed by those epistemologists to whom scientific progress, especially during the last centuries, consists essentially in the discovery of new facts. The entire objective content of knowledge is constituted of empirical data of standardized observation. Scientific systems introduce into this content a formal order which has no objective validity of its own, is entirely arbitrary in the sense that it is neither true nor false. If one system is preferable to another, it is only because it serves better the purposes of intellectual orientation, helps the observer survey a greater number and variety of facts with the same mental effort or the same number and variety of facts with less mental effort. In short, the principle of scientific systematization is purely utilitarian. E. Mach and his followers call it the principle of "economy of thinking."

3. THE DISCOVERER OF PROBLEMS (INDUCTIVE THEORIST) [2]

The development of scientific exploration culminates in the social role of the scientist who, like the discoverer of facts, explores empirical reality but whose self-appointed function is not to find hitherto unknown empirical data but to discover new, hitherto unforeseen *theoretic problems* and to solve them by new theories. And new theoretic problems may concern data which have long been familiar to scientific observers as well as data which have never yet been observed.

We speak of "discovering," not of "raising," new problems. For a theoretic problem is an objective problem of science, not a subjective problem of an individual or a collectivity. Every theoretic problem originates in an application of an objective, rationally standardized theory to an objective, methodically standardized reality, and is solved by an objective modification of the

[2] There is a vast literature bearing upon the matters discussed in this and the next section; nearly all of it, however, is concerned with the sciences of nature and the scientists who have creatively participated in their development. The author has borrowed from so many methodologists, epistemologists, and historians working in this field that it would take a volume to acknowledge all his debts. He owes the most probably to Henri Poincaré.

original theory or by an entirely different theory, also rationally standardized.

The discoverer of problems is not a rebel against scientific rationalism as manifested in theoretic construction: what he rejects is scientific dogmatism, as expressed in the claim that a certain theory contains the only true knowledge about a certain object matter. He is opposed to every kind of dogmatism: the kind which the social milieu imposes upon the theoretic conceptions of technologists and of sages in the name of practical utility; the kind with which a sacred school maintains that its doctrine is the Truth because its source is divine; and the kind which the knowledge of secular scholars derives from the rational evidence of its ontological principles and the formal necessity of its logic. For a dogmatic theory tends to close within the field of its application the way to new theoretic possibilities, whereas the explorer sees new theoretic possibilities in every field he approaches.

Of course, scientific dogmatism can never altogether prevent new theoretic problems from arising: there always have been scientists whose thinking transgressed the limits imposed by a socially immobilized theory. The technologists who went beyond the demands of their social circles in setting new practical problems and risking hazardous solutions were often led to doubt old theoretic certainties on which they were supposed to rely in practice, and they applied instead new theoretic hypotheses of which this very application was to be a test. This has been one of the factors in the gradual disappearance of magical thinking and has resulted in an agglomeration of many specific inductive generalizations, descriptive and causal, concerning inorganic and organic nature which—as recent historians have amply shown—prepared the way for modern science. However, theoretic problematization is only incidental in the performance of the technologist's function and subsidiary to his practical task; if consistently pursued, it would lead him away from his role. Therefore, even such theoretic problems as arise in the course of technological planning and invention are nowadays mostly taken over by theoretic explorers.

Sages also have occasionally raised new theoretic problems and proposed new hypotheses in psychology, sociology, political science, economics, theory of religion; and here also recent history is doing its best to separate such theoretic achievements from their evaluative and normative constructions. But it is not surprising that in their case theoretic problematization is scarce, for it does not merely transcend but actually conflicts with social demands. Whatever is right must be founded on truth, whatever is wrong must be based on error; and since the sage must be perfectly sure of right and wrong, problems of truth and error are solved for him in advance, though it may take a considerable effort of reflection and observation on his part to reach the "proper" solution. And, indeed, we find in the works of sages only such problems openly formulated as they are sure to have already solved in conformity with their ideologies. We often suspect a self-imposed check on new thinking, an unwillingness to face some new problem of which the thinker is probably conscious but which he fears may lead to a solution conflicting with his social philosophy. Thus, the French rationalists of the eighteenth century seem to have been well aware of the problems of irrationality in cultural life but would not study them lest the ideal of a perfectly rational new social order be thereby endangered. Only radical critics of all cultural orders do not hesitate to raise unsolved theoretic problems in this field; but as they are mostly also theoretic skeptics, they do not solve these problems and thus do little to promote positive knowledge.

The pitfall of skepticism has always made scholars afraid of treading the dangerous path of unrestrained new problematization. If truth is absolute, if any knowledge which is not true must be false, and if all the truths about the same object matter are bound together by a systematic order in accordance with the principles of logical deduction, then, after the essential truths within a definite field of knowledge have been discovered and their systematic order has been determined, no further study of this field will raise any *objectively new problems,* that is, problems which cannot be solved by deduction from those essential truths. A problem may be subjectively new to an individual scholar faced with unfamiliar data or unfamiliar aspects of familiar data; but after investigating it, he will find that it either is reducible to problems already solved by the system or is a pseudo-problem—does not concern the object matter upon which the system is bearing.

Of course, both the secularization of knowledge and the foundation of new secular schools involved raising objectively new problems which the old system could not solve, whereas the new system did so. But the basic pattern of the scholar's role made it impossible for him to persist in this innovating type of scientific investigation. Any scholar who opposed a new theory to the theories of his predecessors had to claim for it the same kind of absolute validity which they were supposed to possess and had to prove his claim by rational demonstration. His theory might be still incomplete and its completion left to his followers; but so far as it went, it had to be final. If, while rejecting other theories, he could not or would not use the standards of scholarly knowledge to establish the validity of his own theory, this meant to the scholarly world that he did not recognize those standards, and he was branded a skeptic. And skeptics were not regarded as fit members of a school where truth was taught to the young generation.

It is therefore perfectly understandable from the sociological point of view that even the majority of the great theoretic explorers of the last three centuries have accepted the traditional roles of discoverers of absolute truths and builders of uncontrovertibly valid systems, when such roles were thrust upon them by scholarly circles of contemporaries and successors, since they had been brought up under the scholarly criteria of truth and saw no alternative to these criteria other than a skeptical denial of the objective validity of all theories either in the form of subjectivism or of critical empiricism. While discovering and solving their new problems, they looked toward the future, wandered into the unknown, sought for the unexpected. But when they had to organize systematically the results of their exploration and to justify them theoretically before the community of scientists which kept the scholarly traditions alive, they turned toward the past and accepted as guide its standards of valid theory; or, if they did not, their disciples did it for them. Only a few years ago a scientist, now dead, disciple of a famous theoretic explorer whose system he developed, during an academic celebration on his behalf, proudly said that for thirty years he had found no reason for changing his fundamental theory.[3]

It is no doubt a great honor to be recognized as founder of a new school of scientific thought and to have one's theories accepted as finally and unconditionally true by a faithful body of followers; the very consideration for their trust may be a powerful factor inhibiting further excursions into the unknown in search of new problems—unless one is sure that one's theory will be adequate to deal with them, and then they cannot be objectively new and really unexpected. But apart from social influences, there has been another difficulty in breaking away from the scholarly conception of true knowledge. There is no other form of scientific systematization in existence except the systematization of scientific results. The theoretic explorer has a ready pattern,

[3] De Greef, a disciple of Comte, who supplemented Comte's general classification of sciences by a special classification of social sciences in which the science of economic phenomena is regarded as fundamental.

the old scholarly pattern, for systematizing the *solutions* of theoretic problems; there is no pattern for systematizing *problems*. We mentioned above the university textbook as the kind of work in which scholarly systematization survives. Every textbook, in every field of science, gives primarily a survey of those results of scientific investigation which are regarded as proven, presenting them—as far as possible—in a logical order modeled upon the deductive order of scholarly systems. Problems are given, indeed, for students to solve; but these are either problems which were solved by scientists long ago or else such as can be solved easily with the help of the systematic theory contained in the book; in short, they are patterned upon the kind of problem which scholarly contributors have been solving for over twenty centuries. Some explorers are aware that this type of systematization does not harmonize with their conception of knowledge, but they justify it on educational grounds; and in any case they have not developed any other type to take its place. Consequently, we notice that, in the scientific circles where the search for new problems dominates, systematization is more and more neglected and nearly all scientific work is expressed in monographs.

Under such strong and persistent pressure of the ideals and patterns of scholarship, the liberation of modern theoretic science from scholarly dogmatism is not easy to explain. It may be regarded as a continuation of that historical trend toward freedom of thought which was previously manifested in the struggle of secular against sacred scholars for the autonomy of knowledge.

EXPLORER AND NEW KNOWLEDGE

We saw that the struggle was won because secular scholars mustered organized Reason against organized Faith, opposed a standard of absolute truth founded on the inner rational evidence of knowledge to the standard of absolute truth founded on sacred traditions. Only after religion could no longer control rational science, came the new historical tendency: to make knowledge free to develop in unforeseen directions by breaking the bonds which rational systems constructed by great thinkers of the past laid upon all new thinking. The first step was the emphasis of discoverers of facts upon empirical reality as infinitely rich, varied, and imprevisibly changing, the source of new knowledge in contrast with the dry and rigid schematism of scholarly constructions.

The next step was due perhaps to that general exaltation of creative individualism which since the days of Humanism has gradually permeated all domains of cultural life—art, literature, religion, social and political organization, economic enterprise, material technique. Empirical reality gives the scientist inexhaustible materials for creative thinking; new theories are products of scientific creativeness. This involves a complete rejection of the deductive structure of science which in the scholarly conception of knowledge is essential to its validity. All science is inductive; deduction can serve only as an auxiliary method in raising problems for inductive research, never as the ruling method by which inductive solutions of those problems have to be validated. Inductive science is theoretic science, not mere agglomeration of facts; but its theories must be judged by its own standards of objective validity, which were unknown to scholars.

We may for this reason call the modern discoverer of new problems which he solves by new theories of empirical reality also an "inductive theorist." Nowadays, he is no longer (as his early predecessors were) socially dependent for his scientific status upon the recognition of scholars, who judged his theories by their criteria; he is a participant in a world-wide community of explorers with the same interest in untried theoretic possibilities as he has. He finds the problems he has discovered stimulating them to new research and is stimulated to new research by the problems which they discover.

But—and here lies a subjective difficulty which not every inductive theorist is able to overcome—he becomes aware after a time that his solutions of new objective problems, which he regards as perfectly valid, are not accepted by other explorers in the same spirit as scholarly disciples usually accept the truths discovered by their master. His theory may indeed stir interest, even enthusiasm, but the more important it is, the more widely known and recognized, the greater the stimulus it gives to new problematization. And sooner or later he finds that his theory, often in consequence of the very influence it has had upon the thinking of other scientists, becomes superseded by a new theory.

This is a hard personal test. Will he successfully exclude from his own thought that very tendency to dogmatize which perhaps he, like other explorers, has often condemned in his predecessors? Of course, he will not surrender his theory without a struggle. But what will be the method of this struggle? Will he follow the example of sages, putting forward facts and interpretations which favor it, pushing into shadow facts which furnish arguments against it? Will he use the formal logical method of scholarly "polemics"? Or will he rather try to save his theory by new exploration, modifying and developing it so that it will become fit to solve such new problems as neither he nor his opponents have yet been aware of?

In any case, as the same fortune or misfortune sooner or later befalls every inductive theorist, the community of creative scientists is attempting to develop those standards of theoretic validity which inductive science needs.

There are no absolute, unconditionally certain truths concerning any given object matter of knowledge. There are only truth-hypotheses, with a validity which is dependent on definite conditions. The verification of a hypothesis does not mean that the latter comes nearer to becoming absolute truth with every successful test. It only means ascertaining the range of its validity, determining what are the problems which it can solve. On the other hand, when a hypothesis fails in any particular test, this does not mean that it is false. It only means that we have reached a limit of its validity, discovered a problem which it cannot solve, and that another hypothesis is needed which will solve it, either in conjunction with the first or instead of the first. Experience cannot ultimately prove or disprove any scientific truth, for the facts which we use to test our hypotheses are not the original data of experience but data already selected, reconstructed, and standardized from the point of view of our problems.

A theory is a system of mutually supplementary hypotheses by the aid of which a set of theoretic problems concerning a certain complex of empirical data can be solved. Its validity is only relative, not subjectively relative in reference to the thinker but objectively relative in reference to other theories. It does not depend on the psychological dispositions or biological needs of man, individually or collectively, whether a certain theory furnishes the solution of a certain set of problems or not. He may be uninterested in these problems, or ignorant of the theory, or too stupid to understand it, or too prejudiced to use it: the theory once created is there, an objectively binding norm for any thinking that tries to solve those problems. But it is not the only theory possible about the given complex of empirical data. There may already be or there may be later created other theories that offer different solutions of the same problems, like the Ptolemaic and the Copernican theories in astronomy, the Lamarckian and the Darwinian theories in biology, the theory of parallel independent development and the theory of diffusion in cultural anthropology and so on.

There is no criterion, either logical or empirical, according to which, if one of such different theories be judged true, the other must be judged false. Each may be "true" in the sense that it is consistent in its inner

EXPLORER AND NEW KNOWLEDGE 189

structure and adequate to solve the problems within its range; the difference between their solutions means only that they are making a different use of the same empirical materials, that out of the inexhaustible wealth of the concrete empirical data with which they are dealing, each has selected different elements and relations as scientifically significant for the solution of its problems. But this, again, does not mean that the choice between any given theories is subjectively arbitrary. For there are objective standards by which inductive theories can be compared and their relative validity estimated. Of two theories, A and B, bearing on the same empirical field, if B solves all the problems A has solved and also other problems which A could not solve, B is superior to A in theoretic validity, both from the rational and from the empirical point of view. For, if not more consistent, it is more comprehensive as a system of truth-hypotheses; while the new problems it has raised imply that it has initiated or followed up the discovery of unknown empirical data or of unknown elements and relations among known empirical data which A did not use as scientific material.

But such a comparison between theories as to their relative scientific validity does not exhaust yet the problem of their relationship. Theories do not separately and abstractly subsist in a timeless world of Platonic ideas: they are created and they continue to exist in the course of the historical development of knowledge. The very discovery of objective problems which a certain theory cannot solve would have been impossible if it had not already solved its own previously discovered problems. Its hypotheses have shown explorers the way to new problems by their failure to work beyond the range of their applicability; this is the initial stage of a creative investigation resulting in a more valid theory. Every scientific theory is thus both an end and a beginning; it grows out of a preceding theory which it supplants and becomes the root of a subsequent theory which will supplant it.

According to this conception of scientific knowledge, the function of inductive theorists is to participate in the development of objective scientific thought by creating new systems of relative truths, founded upon less valid systems of their predecessors and serving as foundation for more valid systems of their successors.

4. DIFFERENTIATION AMONG INDUCTIVE THEORISTS

Not all who participate in this creative development of knowledge and reflect about it conceive in the same way the historical significance of their function. Scientists who investigate natural reality, especially those who specialize in physical science, tend to interpret this significance differently from scientist-humanists who explore the empirical realm of cultural data.

The former do not like to resign the guiding ideal of a logically perfect system of absolutely certain rational truths. For their knowledge grows in increasingly close connection with mathematics. And the development of pure mathematics is not subjected to that relativity which characterizes all inductive theoretic knowledge of empirical data. It is neither, as scholarly knowledge claimed to be, deduction of new truths from established truths nor substitution of new systems for old systems but creation of new systems to which old systems become logically reduced. This is because pure mathematics is not knowledge, either in the scholarly or in the modern inductive sense of the term; it has no reference to any object matter beyond itself. It is a growing structure of formal, logically standardized relationships between arbitrary, meaningless signs. Only when these signs are made meaningful by being defined as symbols designating scientific facts, mathematics becomes a symbolic expression of scientific theories. If these are inductive theories, as in modern physics, they are relative, like all inductive knowledge. But some physicists do not accept this distinction between mathematics and physical theories mathematically symbolized. To them mathematical formulas are not mere symbolic expressions of abstract inductive knowledge about empirical facts but constitute knowledge about empirical facts itself. Such a conception is in agreement with the doctrine of those schools discussed in the preceding chapter to whom knowledge is nothing but a system of symbols; consequently, there is a growing coöperation between these physicists and the builders of symbolic logic, who see in theoretic physics that ontological basis of absolutely true knowledge which they themselves cannot discover. According to this mathematicophysical philosophy, the universe in its very essence is a mathematically ordered universe. "God is a mathematician." Every mathematically expressed truth about physical facts is within its own range a fragment of the total absolute truth. If our present physical knowledge as a whole continually changes, showing that it is not yet absolutely certain, this is only because it is incomplete and not yet given a final mathematical systematization. But since we are all the time discovering new physicomathematical truths, the development of our knowledge gradually approaches a perfect and complete mathematical synthesis of the physical universe as an ideal limit. The theoretic explorer appears here as a member of a small and highly select group on its way to absolutely true and all-inclusive knowledge.

This is not how his role is conceived by those investigators of culture who view it historically and compare the history of knowledge with that of other domains of cultural achievement. The linguist, the historian and theorist of literature, the student of art, the religionist, the sociologist, the economist—each finds in the field of his own scientific research many and diverse cultural systems, each of which (just like a system of knowledge) lays claim to some kind of objective validity, though different *in specie* from theoretic validity. A drama, a symphony, a painting, a religious ritual, a bank, an army corps, each has a specific, standardized inner order of its own with which all those comply who participate in it directly or vicariously; this order raises it above the arbitrariness and variability of subjective psychological experiences and impulses.[4]

[4] Perhaps the first origin of the idea that every cultural system has

The scientific explorer of cultural reality overcame long ago the narrow exclusiveness of the sage, who exalts the religion in which he believes as the only really holy religion, the art of his own civilization as the only art which satisfies the supreme canons of beauty, the social structure which he helps promote as the only one that is ethically and politically right, the economic organization for which he and his class stand as the only one that is really conductive to common welfare, and so on. While at first, in reaction against this naïve dogmatism of sages, many investigators of culture went to the other extreme, identified relativity with subjectivity and attempted to reduce the vast and infinitely complex variety of cultural systems to psychological or psychobiological facts, the progress of critical exploration has shown that such an approach leaves most of the theoretic problems concerning culture not only insolvable but undiscoverable. To deny the objectivity of all cultural systems is as naïve in its way as to affirm that only "our" systems are objective.

It is, indeed, a simple way of avoiding the difficulties which an investigator of culture must encounter when he explores the enormous and seemingly chaotic empirical wealth of culture in search not of one order already familiar from personal participation or known from some other science but of many diverse and partial orders theoretically unknown. And, of course, a way which

---

some objective, though only relative, validly must be traced back to the philosophy of Hegel; but, of course, its most important implications have been obscured by Hegel's metaphysical monism and its most fruitful consequences checked by the dogmatic absolutism of his own doctrine.

shows how to play the role of scientist easily will always find many followers. But there are a number of leading scientists in all fields of cultural research who are fully aware of how very difficult the function of inductive theorist is in their fields and who for that very reason eagerly seek new problems. These men are trying to elaborate general heuristic principles which will enable the explorer to take into consideration the various claims to objective validity which all cultural systems have in the experience of the people who participate in them and yet make him maintain his own standards of theoretic objectivity by refraining from evaluative judgments about the data he investigates. Such principles have gradually and independently evolved in the several sciences of culture—and they are essentially similar to those which help the explorer to understand his own role as builder of theoretic systems.

Explorers, as we have seen, are freely promoting and accepting as normal in the domain of knowledge ceaseless and unexpected changes. Such changes are also found in every other cultural field, though not everywhere so rapid or so consciously realized by those who bring them about. If thoroughly and comprehensively investigated, cultural change proves to be a succession of cultural systems constructed according to different patterns, where new systems supplant old ones. And this process can be similarly explained as the succession of theoretic systems. Every cultural system—linguistic, artistic, religious, social, economic, technical—embodies a certain pattern of normatively regulated activities which people follow in solving certain problems which they meet in their lives. Systems vary as to the character and range of problems which can be solved by following their normative patterns. If a certain system proves unfit to solve new problems which arise in the course of historical duration —often in the very consequence of its own expansion— another kind of system becomes substituted instead by the people who are facing these problems.

This, however, does not mean that any one system is ever entirely reducible to another. For even if the new system solves, besides the new problems, all the problems which the old system used to solve—and this is by no means always the case—yet each system solves them differently. Each gives something to human lives which no system built according to a different pattern can give. Forgotten languages, works of art produced in periods long past, ancient religions, old forms of social organization, have been largely supplanted by modern cultural products but not fully absorbed by them; even modern machine technique, which leaves hardly any problems unsolved that hand technique used to solve, is nonetheless not a complete substitute for the latter, since the old patterns of technical action are different from the new. A proof of this irreducibility of earlier culture to later culture in any field is the fact that many old cultural patterns survive the material destruction of old cultural products and continue to be used, though less widely, along with modern patterns; evidently, the solution of certain cultural problems which they give is still satisfactory to some people.

196 EXPLORER AND NEW KNOWLEDGE

Is it not the same in the evolution of knowledge? Among those who believe in absolute truth as the supreme goal which knowledge gradually approaches, the opinion is current that in science—in contrast to art, literature, religion, and social organization—there is a continuous and unreserved "progress" in the sense that anything that was valid in old theories becomes incorporated in new theories and only that which is worthless drops out. But the historian who is accustomed to apply the concept of relative but objective validity to all cultural systems will hardly agree with this opinion. In his view, no system of knowledge is entirely reducible in its theoretic bearing to any other system, however superior the latter may be in its capacity to solve many and various problems. While acknowledging, for instance, that present scientific theories in every branch of knowledge are much more valid relatively than those of Greek philosophers, yet he will not agree that modern thought has made the philosophy of Aristotle or that of Plato utterly insignificant, depriving them of all theoretic validity within the range of those problems which they have solved in their own ways.

Furthermore, recent explorers of cultural reality have discovered that in no field of culture does evolution proceed in one definite direction which could be indicated by some ultimate, supreme limit of the historical process. On the contrary, any cultural system may and often does become the starting point for several different lines of cultural development, each of which leads in turn to

EXPLORER AND NEW KNOWLEDGE

several unexpected possibilities of further evolution in different directions. In the history of knowledge this ceaseless growth of new and divergent lines of theoretic exploration is very clear. The line taken by modern mathematical physics is only one of many, and it may break up sooner or later into several new, now unexpected lines.

Thus viewed in the light of cultural exploration, the relativity of scientific theories cannot be overcome by the acceptance of the ideal of one absolutely valid system of knowledge which is being gradually approached by the double process of creating more and more valid theories and discarding less valid theories of the past. But does not relativism in the field of knowledge, like skepticism, turn against itself and undermine its own claim to be regarded as theoretically valid?

It is not our present task to defend the relativistic conception of theoretic validity but only to show how and why it explicitly or implicitly underlies the theoretic explorer's social role when viewed as that of a creative participant in the historical evolution of culture. However, we can well understand that to combat this conception by the classical arguments invented against skepticism is a superficial quibble of verbal logicians. For those who believe that every theory is relatively valid do not assert that knowledge as a whole has only a relative validity. Theirs is not merely an abstract generalization of some common characters of scientific theories but a synthetic and dynamic view of knowledge as a totality of theoretic systems growing through the ages, each only relatively true, but all of them together embodying a supreme form of validity which the term "truth" in its scholarly meaning is quite unfit to express. There is a parallel conception of art among modern historians and philosophers: each work of art as an aesthetic value is relative, since it solves only some artistic problems among many and satisfies only some aesthetic standards but no others; and yet art as a whole is not relative, for all artistic problems ever perceived find adequate solution in the course of its growth and there are works which satisfy every aesthetic standard.

Such a conception shows the only way to escape the dilemma of dogmatic certainty and skeptical doubt and makes the identification of relativism with subjectivism and objective validity with absolutism impossible. It is undeveloped as yet; indeed, only an inductive nonevaluative science of knowledge, which—as we mentioned in Chapter I—is not yet constituted, will be able to develop it fully. But we can see how, if it be accepted, the social role of the scientist will look in its light.

He is a creator whose work, a unique and irreducible link between the past and the future, enters as a dynamic component into the total, ever-increasing knowledge of mankind. We say, "knowledge of mankind," for it is the knowledge in which all men, from the forgotten beginning to the unknown end of history, have participated and will participate in various ways and degrees. But we do not say "human knowledge." For this knowledge as a whole, in the objective composition and structure of the systems which constitute it, steadily rises far above "human nature" and draws individuals and collectivities after it.

We spoke of the proud claim of the scholar who vindicated the inner dignity of that puny creature—man—asserting his ability to *discover* absolute truth by the unaided effort of his own reason. Cannot the scientist-explorer make the still prouder claim of being one of those who by their coöperative efforts *create* a superhuman world of relative truths, infinite in potential wealth, admirable in its trend to perfection—and who thus lead mankind to undreamed of heights of intellectual achievement?

And perhaps at no period of history was a vindication of the inner dignity of man more needed than in these days.

INDEX

Absolute, The, 146, 161, 198
Adult education, 151
"Adventure" *vs.* scientific exploration, 173
Advisers, occupational, *see* Occupational advisers
Agriculture, 162; experts, 48, 50; inventions and, 57, 61; research, 50-51
Albert the Great, 172
"Aleatory element" (Sumner), 33
Alexandria, 154
Amenophis IV, 72
American Indians, technical knowledge, 25
Americans, ideological conflicts, 81n; social roles, 14, 19
Anderson, Edwin, 4n
Animal husbandry, 162; absurd ideas in, 30; inventions and, 61
Anthropology, and sociology, 136; theories, 188
Arabs, sacred lore, 93
Arbiters, in technological problems, 36
Archimedes, 56
Aristotelians, Christian, 123; Mohammedan, 123
Aristotle, 6, 78, 117, 123, 129, 172, 196
Art, cultural patterns, 87, 192, 194-96; explanation, 168n; modern, 165; relative value, 198; religionistics of, 3; sociology of, 1, 3; standards and norms, 88
Artisans, social roles, 15, 18, 20; technical knowledge, 30-31, 34

Asia, sacred schools in West, 113
Associations, secret, 93-94, 97-98
Assyria, culture, 93
Astronomy, 11; founders, 117; schools in antiquity, 115; theories, 188
Atheism, 81n
Aurelius, *see* Marcus Aurelius
Avicenna, 123
Aztecs, sacred lore, 93

Babylonia, culture, 46; medicine, 35; sacred lore, 93, 104
Bacon, Roger, 56
Bankers, social roles, 14, 15
Barnes, H. E., 68n, 127n
Barry, Frederick, 149
Becker, Howard, 68n, 127n
Behaviorism, 6; validity, 7
Bernal, John Desmond, 82
Berr, Henri, 93n
Bible, 108
Biology, 11, 82, 175; application, 80; of Aristotle, 172; popularization of, 151; systematic, 18, 21; theories, 6, 136, 188
Blackstone, William, 77
Bolshevism, 76; sages and, 73; *see also* Communism; Socialism
Books, popular, 152-53; popular medieval, 152n
Botany, 117
Bourgeois, Der (Sombart), 13
Bruno, Giordano, 174
Buddhism, 95
Buffon, Comte de, 117
Burgess, E. W., 14n

INDEX

Caesar, 72
Calvin, John, 7, 72
Candolle, A. de, 134, 149
Capitalism, 77, 79, 81n
Carnegie, Andrew, 44n
Catholicism, struggle with Protestantism, 74
Cato, 77
Character, words denoting, 16
Chemistry, 11, 44, 117, 175; popularization, 151; research, 51
China, culture, 93; inventions, 58; philosophy of, 78-79; scholars, 92, 99-100, 104
Christianity, 77, 79; function of leaders, 73; and sacred schools, 113; struggle with Paganism, 74; *see also* Sacred schools
Chrysippus, 123
Church fathers, function of, 73
Cicero, 77
Civil engineering, knowledge requirements, 44-45, 162
Civilization, *see* Culture
Classes, social, 2n, 14n, 18
Collectivism, 81n
Commentaries, sacred, 107-9, 112
Commerce, inventions and, 58; schools, 115
Common sense, as basis of social order, 64
Common-sense knowledge, collective opposition to, 68-72; validity, 65-68, 140
Communication, and discovery of new knowledge, 165, 172
Communism, 77, 79, 81n; *see also* Bolshevism; Socialism
Community life, simple, 25, 29-30, 38, 72
Compayré, Jules G., 149
Comte, August, 2, 43, 183n

Conduct, standards and norms, 76-80, 84, 86-88
Conflicts, of ideologies, 68-83 *passim*, 165
Confucius, 77, 95
Conservatives, in social struggle, 70-73, 77
Contradiction, in testing theories, 142-43, 158
Cooley, C. H., 13n
Copernicus, 117, 188
Creators, of new knowledge, 135, 164-99
Cubism, cultural patterns, 7
Culture, 64-90, 111-13, 193; differentiation of roles in, 83-90; evolution possibilities, 89-90, 164-65, 196-97; history, 93n, 164, 173-74; and individualism, 185; irreducibility of earlier to later, 195; and the knowledge of sages, 74; leaders, 87-90, 161; patterns, 19, 20, 68-69, 86, 192, 194-96; personal, 161-62; post-tribal, 93; role of sages in, 72-82; role of scientists in, 82-83, 85, 88-90; science of, 87-90, 192-97; validity of systems, 192n-93; Western, 74
Cynics, 78
Czarnowski, S., 2n

Dante, 77
Darwin, Charles, 6, 188
Deduction, 6, 122, 124-26, 128, 136, 141, 146-47, 148, 167, 172-73, 181, 185, 191
De Greef, G., 183n
Democracy, and intellectual education, 162; sages in a, 81; and theoretic objectivity, 176; *vs.* totalitarianism, 81n
Democritus, 6
Demonstration, rational, 141

INDEX

Descartes, René, 117, 123, 172
Dewey, John, 167-68, 168n
Discoverers, 117-22, 137; of facts, 169-78; of problems, 178-90
Discoveries, priority, 121; validity of, 118-22
Disraeli, Benjamin D., 77
Dogmatism, 198; scholastic, 184; scientific, 179
Duhem, Pierre, 121n
Durkheim, Émile, 2, 4n, 12

Ecclesiastes, Book of, 78
Eclectics, 148-49, 160
Economics, 45; application of, 80; as basis of sociology, 183n; cultural aspects of, 87; knowledge of, 64-65; popularization of, 151; schools of, 136, 175, 180, 192, 194; sociology of, 1; standards and norms, 88
"Economy of thinking," 178
Edison, Thomas, 56
Education, 149-57; in ancient times, 154; modern higher, 126-27, 154-55; of a scholar, 130-35; social function, 155-57; technological, 62; see also Religious schools; Schools; Teachers
Egypt, ancient culture, 46; ancient medicine, 35; sacred lore, 93, 104; sacred schools, 113
Einstein, Albert, 6
Elea, school of, 120
Empiricism, 6, 42, 120, 139-41, 171-72, 174, 185, 188-90, 193; critical, 182; scientific standardization, 140, 176-77; social, 87
Ends and means, of cultural life, 83-90
Engineering, 162; progress, 46; see also Civil engineering
Epicure, 117

Epistemology, 4, 10, 120, 136, 142, 145, 177, 178n
Erasmus of Rotterdam, 73
Ethics, norms, 20; rebellion against, 175; sacred, 108
Ethnography, 175
Etruscans, sacred lore, 93
Evolution, 136
Experience, and scientific truth, 187; social origin, 2
Experimentation, technological, 49-51
Experts, statistical, 49, 50; technological, see Technological experts
Exploration, scientific, 62, 164-99

Fabre, F., 173
Fact-finders, scientific, 169-78
Factory workers, classification, 18
Facts, certainty of, 177
Faith, 185
Family, social roles, 14-15
Faris, E., 2n
Farmers, social roles, 14, 16, 18, 20; technical knowledge, 25, 30, 34
Fechner, Gustav T., 117
Fénelon, François, 77
Fichte, J. G., 146
Fleming, Arthur Percy Morris, 62n
Folkways (Sumner), 33
Fontana, Giovanni de la, 56
France, culture in Middle Ages, 152n; prestige of academicians, 92
Frazer, J. G., 13, 34n
Freedom, intellectual, 159, 184
Freud, Sigmund, 117

Galen, 56, 117
Galilei, Galileo, 117
Gauls, sacred lore, 93

INDEX

Generalizations, inductive, *see* Induction
Geography, 136, 175; experts, 48
God, 79, 109, 112-13, 191
Golden Bough, The (Frazer), 13
Gomperz, T., 149
Good and evil, 79, 84
Granet, Maurice, 79n, 149, 160
Greece, culture, 127n, 154, 174; medicine in, 35; originator of rationalism, 120; sacred lore, 93; sacred schools, 113; science, 108
Grote, G., 149
Guidance, vocational, 13

Halbwachs, Maurice, 2n
Hebrews, orthodox, 92-93; sacred schools, 113; sacred texts, 104
Hegel, G. W., 117, 123, 160, 193n
Heredity, 18, 21
Heron, of Alexandria, 56, 58
Hiller, E. T., 14n
Hippocrates, 117
Historians, 148-49, 178n, 196-98
History, research in, 175; schools of, 136, 192
Hitler, Adolf, 72
Hubert, H., 94n
Humanism, 185, 190
"Humanistic coefficient," in sociological investigation, 5, 6, 7, 12
Humanists, function of, 73
Human Nature and the Social Order (Cooley), 13n
Hume, David, 78
Hunters, technical knowledge, 25, 28, 34
Huxley, J. G., 83n

"Idea," definition, 8
Ideologies, construction, 83-90; of sages, 76-80; social roles and, 14; struggle of, 68-83 *passim*

Ideology and Utopia (Mannheim), 2n
Impressionism, cultural patterns, 7
Incas, sacred lore, 93
India, sacred lore, 93, 104; sacred schools, 113
Individualism, 81n; creative, 185
Individuals, classification, 14, 15; cultural activities, 11; evaluation, 67; social roles, *see* Social roles
Induction, 6, 42-43, 127-29, 140, 167, 169, 172, 180, 185, 191, 198; theoretic, 178-99
Industrialists, American, 44n
Inferiority, personal, 66
Initiation, to sacred societies, 93-94, 98
Innovators, *see* Inventors; Novationists; Scientists
Instruments, scientific, 176
Intelligence, words denoting, 16
Internationalism, 81n
Inventions, 52-64, 180; attributes, 52-54; as cultural and practical phenomena, 52; of early times, 57-58; of patterns of technical action, 51-54; of playthings, 58; technological growth of, 56, 60-61; technological restriction, 55-58, 60-61
Inventors, amateur, 56; coöperation among, 60-61; with technological leaders, 62; with theoretic investigators, 62; independent, 55-64, 164; social role and status, 56-60, 80; as teachers, 62
Italy, sacred schools, 113

James, William, 168n
Jews, *see* Hebrews

INDEX

Kant, I., 78, 117, 146
Kepler, J., 117
Kings, social roles, 13, 15
Knowledge, amateur, 152-53; common-sense, 64-83, 140; creators of, 164-99; cultural, *see* Culture; defined by theoretician, 197-98; disseminators, 149-57; economics of, 3; evolution of, 196; historical development, 164, 189; holy, *see* Sacred lore; ideal of religious scholars, 110-11; of mankind, 198-99; personal, 30; philosophy of, 4; popularizers of, 150-53, 166; psychology of, 167; sacred, *see* Sacred lore; scholastic, 175 (*see also* Scholars; Schools of thought); science of, 4; secularization, *see* Schools, secular; sociology of, 1-25, 69-72; systematization of, 122-27, 129, 137, 141, 146, 158, 165, 167-68; systems of, *see* Schools of thought; technical, *see* Technical knowledge; theoretical, 80, 87-90, 151-63 *passim;* theoretical *vs.* practical, 80, 91-92, 162-63; types in simple communities, 25
Knowledge for What? (Lynd), 82

Lamarck, J., 188
Langlois, Charles Victor, 152n
Language, cultural patterns, 7, 87, 192, 194-95; knowledge of, 64; schools in antiquity, 115; sociology of, 1, 3; standards and norms, 88; valuation, 7
Lao-tse, 78
La Rochefoucauld, François, Duc de, 78
Lavoisier, A. L., 117
Law, 162; norms, 19; schools in antiquity, 115; sociology of, 1
"Law of three states" (Comte), 2
Lawyers, social roles, 14
Leaders, social, 72-83; technological, *see* Technological leaders
Leader-thinkers, 72-83
Leisure, and knowledge acquisition, 152-53
Lenin, N. (Ulianow), 72
Le Roy, Édouard, 167
Lévy-Bruhl, Lucien, 2n
Linnaeus, 117
Literature, 196; cultural systems, 192; sociology of, 1
Locke, J., 8, 78
Logic, 4, 128, 137-38, 143-44, 146, 179, 187-88, 190, 197; symbolic, 145-48, 167, 191; *see also* Deduction; Induction; Postulates; Propositions; Rationalism; Reduction
Lore, sacred, *see* Sacred lore
Lumpenproletariat, 77
Lynd, Robert S., 82

Mach, E., 178
Machiavelli, 84-85
Magic, disappearance of, 179-80; empirical criteria, 140; knowledge of, 64; role in practical occupations, 29, 30, 33; sacred, 94, 102, 112, 114
Maistre, Joseph de, 70
Mandarins, social status, 92-93
Mannheim, Karl, 2, 4n
Marcus Aurelius, 78
Marxism, 79
Materialism, 81n, 136
Mathematics, 11, 82; and rational certainty, 120-21, 146, 190-92, 197; schools in antiquity, 115
Mauss, Marcel, 2, 94n
Mayas, sacred lore, 93

Mead, G. H., 14n
Means and ends, of cultural life, 83-90
Mechanics, inventions and, 61
Medicine, 162; ancient, 115; founders, 117; inventions and, 54, 57, 61; research, 50; schools of, 136; *see also* Physicians
Medicine man, 28, 30, 94
Memory, sociological approach, 2n
Men, rating compared to women, 66
Merchants, social roles, 14-15, 18, 20
Method of Sociology (Znaniecki), 5n, 21n
Methodology, 4, 136, 169, 178n
Middle Ages, culture, 93, 152n; logic practiced, 129; sacred lore, 104; sacred schools, 113
Military art, inventions and, 57
Military experts, 48
Military schools, 115
Mill, J. S., 167
Mind, qualities of, 16
Mining, experts, 48; progress, 46
Mohammedans, 123; sacred schools, 113; sacred texts, 104
Monism, 193n
Montaigne, M. de, 78
Morgan, J. Pierpont, 44n
Moses, 72
Mussolini, Benito, 72

Nationalism, 81n
Natural science, 173, 178n
Nauka Polska (Polish Science), monographs on science of knowledge, 5n
Naville, Ernest, 167
Nazism, 74, 76; sages and, 73
Near East, sacred lore under Islam, 104

Newton, Sir Isaac, 6, 117, 123, 158
Nietzsche, Friedrich, 78
Novationists, in social struggle, 70-74, 76, 77; values and tendencies, 76
Numa Pompilius, 72

Oath, of doctor of philosophy, 100n
Observation, 122; scientific, 176; technological, 49-50
Occam, W., 117
Occupational advisers, 31-38; early varieties, 33-38, 57; lay, 35-38 (*see also* Technologists); priests as, 33-35
Occupational patterns, 27, 28, 31, 33, 57
Occupational performance, authorities, *see* Occupational advisers, Technological experts, Technological leaders; disturbances, 31-33; magical beliefs in, 29-30; personality traits as a factor in, 29; truths tested through, 26, 28
Occupational roles, stages, 25-31; training for, 163
Odysseus, 35
Ornstein, Marthe, 56n, 152n
Ostwald, Wilhelm, 134

Paganism, struggle with Christianity, 74
Paracelsus, 56
Park, R. E., 14n
Parmenides, 117, 119
Patterns, cultural, 19, 20, 68-69, 86, 192, 194-96; occupational, 27-28, 31, 33, 57; technological, 51-54
Pearce, J. G., 62n
Peasants, *see* Farmers

INDEX

Peripatetic school, 123
Persia, sacred lore, 93, 104
Personal roles, *see* Social roles
Petrarch, 73
Philology, *see* Language
Philosophers, 167; of culture, 87-88, 198; Greek, 196; *see also* Sages
Philosophy, 100*n*, 123, 145-46, 175; of knowledge, 4, 89, 158; liberation from religious control, 115; relation to social structure, 2; schools, 135-36, 154
Philosophy, Chinese, 78-79
Philosophy, mathematicophysical, 191-92
Physicians, priests as, 35; social roles, 14-15, 18, 20; *see also* Medicine
Physics, 11, 44, 82; application, 80; founders, 117, 123; popularization, 151; and rational certainty, 190-92, 197; systems of, 6, 136, 175
Picard, J., 121*n*, 168*n*
Plato, 6, 8, 78-79, 117, 119, 123, 129, 176, 189, 196
Plotinus, 119
Pneumatica (Heron of Alexandria), 58
Poetry, modern, 165; sacred lore as, 112
Poincaré, Henri, 178*n*
Poland, prestige of professors, 92; university education, 131-33
Polemics, 136-37, 143-44, 187
Polish Sociological Review, 14*n*
Political science, 180; 18th-century French leaders, 73; rebellion against, 175; schools of, 136, 176
Politics, inventions and, 57
Pompilius, *see* Numa Pompilius

Postulates, 146
Preliterate peoples, thinking socially conditioned, 2*n*
Priests, as occupational advisers, 33-35; as physicians in ancient times, 35; social roles, 13, 15, 18, 20, 94-95; sociological study of, 13; *see also* Religious scholars
Primitive peoples, thinking socially conditioned, 2*n*
Primitive Sacred Societies (Webster), 93*n*
Primitive thought, 2*n*
Prince, The (Machiavelli), 84-85
Principle of "economy of thinking," 178
"Private docent," 132
Problems, discoverers of, 178-90; systematization, 184; technical, 36, 37
Professions, technical and social requirements, 9
Prophets, 95, 109, 119
Propositions, 142-44
Protestantism, function of leaders, 73; struggle with Catholicism, 74
Psychologists, 167
Psychology, 45, 65, 192-93; encroachment upon sociology, 1; of knowledge, 167; popularization of, 151; schools of, 6, 117, 136, 172, 175, 180; *see also* Behaviorism; Voluntarism
Psychotechnics, development, 13
Ptolemy, 117, 188
Pythagoras, 117, 119, 121

Rationalism, 29, 120-22, 124-25, 141; 18th-century French, 181; scientific, 179
Reactionaries, in social struggle, 70-71

INDEX

Reality, 146; cultural, *see* Culture
Reason, 146-47, 185, 199
Reduction, 141, 172
Reformation, 73-74
Relativism, 190, 193, 197-98
Religion, 180; cultural aspects, 87; history, 93n, 94n; inventions and, 57; knowledge of, 64-65; rebellion against, 175; role in practical occupations, 33-34; schools of, 136, 192, 194-96; sociology of, 1, 3, 14; standards and norms, 88; struggles of, 73-74, 81n, 185
Religious scholars, 34, 93, 98-116, 119, 125, 158-59, 184; commentaries, 107-9; contribution to knowledge, 110-13; empirical criteria, 140; functions, 102-5, 109; as learners, 100; social roles, 98-99; specialization, 104; as teachers, 101, 149
Religious schools, *see* Sacred schools
Renaissance, 74
Research, cultural, 194; scientific, 62, 89, 166; technological, 48-51
Research in Industry (Fleming and Pearce), 62n
Revolt, against cultural order, 69; intellectual, 169-70, 174-76
Rey, Abel, 149, 160, 168n
"Right," interpretations, 70, 75, 78, 180
Ritual, 102, 112
Rochefoucauld, *see* La Rochefoucauld
Rockefeller, John D., 44n
Roman Catholic Church, *see* Catholicism
Romans, sacred lore, 93
Romanticism, 74
Russell, Bertrand, 82

Sacred lore, 93, 121; growth, 104-5, 107; as a hindrance to social adaptation, 112; interpretation, 107-11; memorizing, 104; transmission, 95-98, 100, 104, 149; validity, 96, 113-15, 118
Sacred schools, 91-116, 118-19, 127, 139, 141, 174-75, 179; conflicts, 105, 113-14; contacts between, 113; famous scholars, 118-19; origin, 93-94; rivalry between, 113-14; standards, 99-100; support, 98
Sages, 72-83, 95, 100, 114, 118, 125, 127, 151, 170, 174-75; as aids to technologists, 86-87; Chinese, 78-79; Christian, 76, 79; as conservatives, 73, 77, 179; defined, 87; function, 72-74, 83, 86-87, 109; ideals and standards, 76-80, 83, 87, 164; knowledge of, 74, 80, 82; method of, 74-75, 138, 140, 171, 187, 193; as novationists, 73, 168, 180; scholars as, 78; scientists as, 80-81; social demand for, 80-82; social status, 91; *see also* Philosophers; Scholars
St. Augustine, 76
St. Thomas, 6, 78, 123, 172
Scheler, Max, 2
Schelting, Alexander von, 4n
Scholars, 91-163, 166, 170-71; as contributors, 127-35, 137, 139, 145, 164-65, 168; as discoverers of truth, 117-22, 127, 137, 139, 145, 168, 170, 182; as disseminators of knowledge, 149-57; distinction between sacred and secular, 116-17; as eclectics, 148-49, 160; as fighters for truth, 128, 135-48, 174; as historians, 148-49; modern education, 130-35; as popularizers of knowledge, 150-

INDEX

53, 166; religious, *see* Priests, Religious scholars; as sages, 78; secular, 113-63, 141, 158-59, 163, 171, 184-85; social roles, 82; as systematizers, 122-27, 129, 137, 145, 167-68; as teachers, 125-26, 151, 153-57; theoretical knowledge, 62, 179; *see also* Sages

School, popular meaning, 154

Schools, American, 154; modern, 115, 154; religious, *see* Sacred schools; sacred, *see* Sacred schools; secular, 113-63, 139, 141, 182

Schools of thought, 3-10, 88, 91-165, 192; defense of, 135-48; defined, 145; diversity, 136; founders, 117-23, 172; historical function, 160-61; social standing, 138; standards of validity, 5-8, 12, 119-22, 124-30, 135-39, 140, 165; struggles between, 136-48, 175, 184-85; *see also* Culture; Knowledge

Science, borderlands of, 1; classification, 183n; creative, 164-99 *passim;* cultural aspects, 87; defined, 146-47; Greek, 108; history of, 134; of knowledge, 9, 11-12, 168, 177, 180, 184, 196; and modern civilization, 83n; popularization of, 151; of sciences, 4, social, *see* Sociology; social function, 82-83; specialization in, 143-44; standards and norms, 88; systems, 3, 136-48, 167, 177-78, 183; textbook, 184

Science and Social Needs (Huxley), 83n

Scientific societies, role in 17th century, 56n

Scientists, 117-22, 134n, 160-61; as creators of new knowledge, 62, 135, 164-99; defined, 11-12; as fact-finders, 169-78; as humanists, 190; as inductive theorists, 178-90; of 19th century, 172; obligations to society, 82; origin of, 91; as sages, 80-81; social, *see* Sociologists; social roles, 21-23, 64, 82, 83, 85, 88, 91-92, 118, 164-65, 167, 178, 198; theoretic, 62; in totalitarian states, 85

Scott, Howard, 82

Seneca, 77

Shils, Edward, 2n

Skepticism, 181-82, 197-98

Skill, technical, 33

Social Actions (Znaniecki), 69n

Social circles (common bond with social person), 14, 15, 21

Social classes, role, 14n, 18

Social function, defined, 17

Social Function of Science, The (Bernal), 82

Social groups, 3, 14n, 66; knowledge requirements, 9

Socialism, 74, 176; 19th-century leaders, 73; *see also* Bolshevism; Communism

Social leaders, 72; *see also* Sages; Technological leaders

Social life, conflicts in modern, 81; dependence on knowledge, 2, 8, 64-65, 155-57; and religious struggles, 74

Social person, 14-17, 21

"Social relation," 3

Social roles, 13-22, 164-65; classes, 14n, 18; components, 17; defined, 13, 19; knowledge as prerequisite, 23-25; limitations, 16; patterns, 19-20; personal qualities, 15-17; of sages, 72-83, 165; of scientists, 21, 22, 64, 82-83, 122-35, 164; of teachers, 24; of technological leaders, 40-41, 82; values, 14-15

INDEX

Social status, defined, 16-17
Social struggle, 68-71, 73-74
Social systems, characteristics, 3; cultural patterns, 19, 192, 194-96; standards and norms, 88; uniformities, 18-19, 21; valuation of, 4-6
Social Thought from Lore to Science (Barnes and Becker), 68n, 127n
Societies, scientific, 56n; secret, 93-94, 97-98
Society, cultural contacts, 68n, 69; cultural history, 93; differentiation of functions, 12; norms of culture, 65-67; technological leadership, 38-47; totalitarian, 73-74, 76, 80, 81n
Sociologists, knowledge of, 64; social roles, 63-64; valuative judgments, 5-8
Sociology, 45, 65, 162; application, 80; of art, 1, 3; borderland problems, 1, 22; classification, 183n; cultural aspects, 87; imperialistic tendencies, 1; and knowledge, 1-25, 69-72; of language, 1; popularization of, 151; of religion, 1; retrogression of scientific, 83; schools of, 136, 172, 175, 180; science of, 4-5, 63; scope, 3; technological progress, 63-64; vs. theory of knowledge, 4
Socrates, 78-79, 119
Solon, 72
Sombart, W., 13
Sophists, 78
Sorcery, 58
Soul, 16, 113
Soziologie, Handwörterbuch der (Vierkandt), 2n
Space, sociological approach, 2n

Specialists, 25-31; study of, 12-14; *see also* Occupational advisers; Scientists; Technological experts; Technologists
Specialization, aspects, 12; scientific, 143-44
Spencer, Herbert, 12, 123, 172
Spinoza, B., 78
Spiritualism, 81n, 136
Statesmen, as leader-thinkers, 72
Statistical experts, role of, 49, 50
Students, desire for certain knowledge, 125-27
"Subject," 146
Subjectivism, 182, 193, 197-98
Sumner, W. G., 33
Sun-Yat-Sen, 72
Superiority, personal, 66
Surgery, *see* Medicine
Symbols, sacred, 95, 102-4, 106, 141; scientific, 141-45, 191
Systematization, of knowledge, 122-27, 129, 137, 141, 146, 158, 167-68, 177-78, 183; of problems, 184

Taine, H., 168n
Teachers, as inventors, 62; social roles, 14, 24
Technical actions, new patterns, 51-54
Technical knowledge, 25-31; as basis of technical skill, 33; cultural patterns, 194; practical application, 25-31; validity tests, 26, 29, 31, 140; diagnosis, 36-37; solution by planning, 37
Technical skill *vs.* technical knowledge, 33
Technological experts, 47-55, 57, 164, 170; inventions by, 52-55; relation to leaders, 47-48, 54-55;

INDEX

research, 48-51; social function, 51, 54, 55, 80, 170-71
Technological knowledge, beginnings of, 31-37; coöperation with philosophy of culture, 89; intellectual leadership by priests, 33-34; progress, 62, 63, 164; social, 1, 3, 84-85; standards and norms, 88; theoretical, 62; in totalitarian states, 85; *see also* Scientists; specialists; Technological experts; Technological leaders; Technologists
Technological leaders, 38-47, 48-49, 54-55, 57, 91, 164, 170; knowledge requirements, 41-46; progress of, 46; relation to experts, 47-48, 54-55; relation to sages, 86; scientific functions, 38-40; social roles, 40-41, 45-47, 80, 86-87, 170
Technological roles, 38
Technological schools, modern, 115
Technologists, 35-64, 76, 88, 100, 114, 118, 125, 127, 151, 166, 168, 174, 179; in cultural realm, 84-90; defined, 36; function, 31-64 *passim*, 83-84, 109, 180; *see also* Inventors; Technological experts; Technological leaders
Technology, *see* Technological knowledge
Textbook, university, 127, 184
Thales, 6, 56, 119
Theology, 115
Theories, validity, 178-99 *passim*
Theorists, inductive, 178-99
Theory, defined, 188
Thinkers, leader-, 72-83
Thoreau, H. D., 173
Thorndike, Lynn, 149

Thought, creative, 164-99 *passim;* development of, 160; freedom of, 159, 184; primitive, 2n; scientific, 167-68; social origin, 2
Time, sociological approach, 2n
Totalitarianism, 73-74, 76, 80, 81n, 85
Toys, inventions of early times, 58
Traits, personality, 29; psychological, 16
Trotsky, Leon, 72
Truth, absolute, 91-163 *passim*, 181, 185, 192, 196, 199; as norm of thinking, 8
"Truth-hypothesis," 187, 189
Truths, common-sense, 66; discovery by secular scholars, 117-22; empirical criterion, 140; as interpreted by sages, 75, 78-79, 180; nature of, 7-8, 198; objective theoretic, 79; relative, 190, 193, 197-98; sacred, 94, 103, 105-9, 114, 179; scientific, 82, 187; secular criteria, 114-15; self-evident, 124, 127; in technical knowledge, 26, 28; in technological leadership, 44-45; testing, 127-30

Universities, European, 130-34, 154; evolution in the West, 115

Validity, common-sense, 66-67, 193; negative, 6-7; standards for new social order, 70; of systems of knowledge, 4-7, 12, 183; theoretic, 6, 137, 178-99 *passim*
Veblen, T. B., 83n
Vierkandt, A., 2n
Vocational guidance, development, 13
Voluntarism, validity of, 7

Warfare, *see* Military . . .
Watt, James, 56
Webster, H., 93*n*
Winchester, Marquis of, 56
Windelband, Wilhelm, 149
Wirth, Louis, 2*n*
Women, rating compared to men, 66
Words, as expression of knowledge, 141-44
Workers, social roles, 14, 18
Writings, early, 103; of leader-thinkers, 72; sacred, 97-98; 103-4

"Wrong," interpretations of, 70, 75, 78, 180
Wundt, W., 123, 167, 172

Xenophanes, 119
Xenophon, 77

Zeller, E., 149
Zeno of Elea, 120
Zeno the Stoic, 117, 123
Znaniecki, F., 5*n*, 14*n*, 21*n*, 69*n*
Zoölogy, 117